Dear God:
Do You Know Any Plumbers Named Shorty?

John Baker

Pebble Creek Press

ISBN 0-9711473-0-2

To Andrew:
May God grant you wisdom
and courage as you reach toward
the potential within you.

Acknowledgments

Debra, my wife, showed patience and gave encouragement, both of which I needed in significant amounts.
However this adventure turns out, I think we've both
learned something from it.

Johnny Aiken, my friend and my coworker, was the first
person outside my family to see the words that follow.
He provided encouragement that he didn't know I
needed when I needed it most.

Paul Moore, my friend and my pastor, has taught me
many valuable lessons about life by the way he lives his
life. Thanks for practicing what you preach.

Betty Templeton, the English teacher who awakened
me to the power of words, and who, along with Charlie,
her husband, gave the final manuscript a going over I
haven't experienced since her English class.

Contents

Introduction

I'm after some basic truth by which to live my life. I have now lived long enough to understand that basic truths exist. If you put your hand on a glowing stove-top burner, your hand will be burned. Buying any stock at its all-time low will drive it to new all-time lows. Cats will mess up your house in some foul way given the opportunity; motive doesn't matter. These few unalterable facts are basic truths, verifiable over the course of human experience.

But, there's one basic truth that has eluded general agreement among people throughout recorded history. That basic truth is the existence and nature of God. Neither stove-tops, cats, nor the secrets of the stock market come close to the uproar caused by a divine Creator. While injuries and even deaths can be attributed to each of these three examples of basic truth, none has sparked the rancor, the bitterness, or the ongoing destruction of lives that occur over and in the name of God.

I grew up as a Christian, more specifically as a Baptist, even more specifically as a Southern Baptist. Baptists, in general, can be a cantankerous lot. They came into being by disagreeing with a *de facto* state church in several of the colonies of what would become the United States. Southern Baptists came into being in a split with their Northern counterparts over slavery.

In my first two, almost three decades of Southern Baptist belief, it was a harmonious way to religious experience. Well-organized programs, entrenched systems of belief, and traditions of worship that everyone knew and responded to appropriately were the hallmarks of my childhood through my mid-20's.

But something happened that affected the way I viewed my faith. Southern Baptists got into another fight, one sometimes fought in the open but more often fought in what would have been smoke-filled back rooms had a local political machine been at stake, rather than a religious denomination.

As I became aware of the struggle and watched it continue, I was forced to consider to which side of the fence I should jump. In that sense, the growing split became a decisive moment in my life. I could have downplayed the whole chain of events, squarely and unknowingly straddling the fence. Most Baptists have, but that wasn't to be my case.

The claims of both sides in this debate forced me to consider what I believed and why I held those beliefs. Because I was reaching toward my thirties when the debate became really nasty and because I had married and had a child, I began to take life and my faith a bit more seriously. The responsibility of marriage and parenting proved serious business. I began to find that life could be painful and was more complex than I'd ever dreamed. I had a good reason to be interested in what I believed and why.

What I found as I began to explore my faith over the last decade is that there are many questions of my religious experience I might never have questioned had these issues not been thrown at me. All of the questions circled eventually to one basic theme: the existence and nature of God, particularly God's relationship with people.

What I found changed my way of looking at the world, for I recognized I had many concepts of God that were cultural as much as scriptural. That the Jesus in whom I professed my belief lived a life much different than what the modern church often prescribes through its actions and attitudes. I became painfully aware that, to follow in the real tradition of Jesus, my life needed to change in some very meaningful ways.

The first two bits of knowledge I gained were intellectual, a mental stimulus registering through the connection of ideas to brain tissue. The last bit of knowledge required changes in behavior, changes which were difficult and even now seem impossible for a frail human spirit.

What I learned was that most of my belief system was ingrained from birth onward through the reinforcement of parents, teachers, and religious leaders. I had to admit I wasn't any different in that respect from a child raised in a Muslim or Jewish tradition. But being Baptist, I'd never given any thought to Muslims or Jews when there were Methodists, Presbyterians, and even Catholics, to contend with on my own turf.

I don't regret that I was led down this particular path, primarily by my parents because I think they've gotten it right. I'm a product of a mixed marriage. My mother is Baptist while my Father is Methodist. My mother won the right early on to take my sister and me to church with her. In either case, I can't find fault in the way they have lived their lives or the system of belief within which they've lived it. People who know my folks would agree.

They lived, however, in a world where questioning answers, from parents or other authority figures wasn't acceptable, while I grew up in a world where a lot of things were open for discussion, which is what Southern Baptists are fighting over now, or were anyway.

What I've found is that some of the answers provided in my religious upbringing don't square with the overall image of God presented in the Bible. I haven't found that God has gotten it wrong. I have found that people have gotten it wrong by applying God the way they want God applied.

I've said all of these things to explain why this introduction and how the letters that follow came to be. In November of 1999, my son came home with a school assignment. He was to write a letter to God, asking any questions he wanted to ask. I don't remember the three or four questions he posed except one, "Is it all right with you if people hunt when they don't need the food?"

Because I had been paid to spend a good bit of my time writing as a marketing type for several businesses in the past, and wasn't spending much time writing in my newest job, I thought asking those types of questions would allow me to do more searching while I received a little writing practice.

I decided to write a letter a week for a year, asking anything I wanted to ask. My original list of questions numbered about ten, which I completed. From there, I've gone on to write the others included here. I haven't been as steady as I vowed to be. I missed one week early on, and, as summer rolled around and my job responsibilities heated up, I was both too tired and too distracted to stay consistent.

But I kept plugging away because I made a commitment to see my assignment through, and perhaps, more importantly, because several people who read them, thought they were pretty good stuff. Others who read them weren't amused, moved, or anything else by them, but that's OK. I wrote them for me and, by extension, for those who want their faith to be a significant part of their life, but don't always agree with everything they've been told.

You may find some of these amusing. You may not.

You may find some poignant, but I doubt it. Poignant isn't one of my strengths.

I hope you'll find all of them thought provoking, in small or perhaps big ways. Wander as each letter may around a subject, each one circles back to the idea that if God is in everything in some form or fashion, everything is worth considering in light of how it reflects God.

I still don't know the answers, though I've attempted a few in how I view God and God's relationship to people. I've grown from asking the questions, even those that seem patently ridiculous compared to the majesty I've always assumed of God.

The letters are unabashedly Christian in their perspective because that is what I know and believe. I don't apologize for that perspective. It's the one I claim. Perhaps if you believe nothing or hold beliefs about God's nature that don't agree with my view at all, you'll still find some idea worth taking away.

Happy reading.

Dear God:
Do you know any plumbers named Shorty?

There seem to be a lot of plumbers named Shorty. Are there?

I'm sure that, even with the extensive work done through the U.S. Census, there's no hard data on this question. At least I don't recall the last census asking for any nicknames I might admit. And I'll bet if it did, Shorty wasn't on the list the Census Bureau compiled. It is a nickname today that would be considering degrading, not that Darrell the Vertically Challenged Plumber would be much of a compliment.

I bring this question to your attention, God, because you are the preeminent statistical authority. Since you have an accurate count of the number of hairs on our heads, even with the growing popularity of Rogaine® and weaves, you'd likely have a fix on any preponderance of plumbers called Shorty.

Speaking from my limited perspective, I assume since plumbing often involves getting under houses and into tight spaces, people whose stature fits the nickname might be in high demand in the plumbing profession. Of course, contradictory evidence suggests that there are an equal number of people with the nickname Shorty who happen to be 6'5" and have never plumbed a day. But that's not what I'm asking.

It might be that the nickname Shorty, as opposed to Jay or Trip or Trey, isn't a nickname of descendency but rather a colloquial working-class title. This difference would suggest that plumbers generally don't consider the gravity of their blood lines in choosing a profession, or it could mean that people named Jay or Trip or Trey don't see plumbing as a fitting realization of their nicknames.

In either case, it makes me wonder why we assume someone named Shorty will more often be a plumber rather than, say, a securities analyst, whatever a securities analyst does. I also wonder why we would generally assume a Shorty is likely to be less intelligent, less likely to subscribe to *Conde Nast* or to consider the merits of Cabernet Sauvignon versus Merlot on a regular basis rather than a Jay or a Trip or a Trey.

I could make a biblical inquiry about this matter, but I'm pretty sure I won't find many nicknames laced throughout the Good Book. Admittedly, you gave Jesus quite a few names to express the range of his being, but I don't think we're talking apples and apples with that comparison.

It may be that the Hebrew writers communicated in a language where every name meant something. Of course, they didn't have soap opera characters from which to draw names for their children, but I suppose we can excuse that slip. I just haven't heard the Hebrew/Aramaic/Greek name for Shorty unless, of course, it's Zacchaeus.

Zacchaeus, at least to my knowledge, was one of the few, if not the only person in the Bible, specifically singled out for lack of height. The Bible is certainly full of people singled out for lack of faith, but I don't know of anyone else noted for possessing a lack of physical stature.

We could conjecture, as we tend to do with the Bible anyway, that Zacchaeus' lack of vertical attainment led to his profession of revenue collector for the government so that he could extract respect via his job title. We could also speculate that no one is named Zacchaeus today because the name carries the liability of an undersized parasite feeding on his own people.

Of course, in our assessment, we'd likely overlook the fact that Jesus took Zacchaeus into his flock, which should tell us that your interest in us goes a bit further than nicknames and job descriptions. It might also be noted that since Jesus didn't exactly accumulate a great deal of material wealth during his stay here, he didn't have need for Zacchaeus' assistance with tax issues, which once again flies in the face of getting the most out of our daily associations with others. But I'm digressing.

I'm curious as to whether you see the Shorty's of the world the same way we do. Do you have a name-by-name profile that says, for example, "Shorty, likely to be a plumber or an HVAC technician. Great manual dexterity, good mind for mechanical solutions, not likely to have read most of the Old Testament or those dumbfounding letters to all those Greek churches?"

Does your profile also read that Shorty is, in general terms, a family man and that he has some pursuits like hunting, fishing and watching Braves baseball (or Pirates, Cubs, Dodgers) that occupy his spare time? Does your profile show Shorty having a receding hairline, a slight lack of confidence and the resulting need to continually prove himself? You don't use the word Napoleon in your profiles, do you?

Would your profile show that Shorty might well be a major league candidate for church membership, especially if the church building has some plumbing needs? And, would your profile suggest that Shorty be given the clear facts about what is expected of faith in you, and then led continually from that point forward to have the resulting conclusions drawn for him?

I wonder these things because I know lots of Shorty's, whether that's their name or not. They're dependable, and loyal, and have a genuine love for college or pro teams or hunting or fishing. The Shorty's I know are amazed their children are as smart as they are and want their children to have a better life than they've had, even though they think their lives have turned out pretty well.

15

Frankly, I'm not sure that the Shorty's of the world don't live far better than the rest of us.

But, I am pretty sure that, if you are who I think you are, the name Shorty doesn't ring any particular bell with you, and it's not, of course, because your residence has no plumbing needs. I doubt the name Shorty has a lot of meaning to you because I suspect you measure things differently than we do.

Since you don't need to read *Conde Nast* to understand the travel implications of any particular destination, I suspect you also see Shorty as one of the total world full of people whom you love. I just wish the Shorty's of the world who haven't heard you love them as much as the more conspicuous among us could get the message without having it filtered by the more conspicuous among us. I'm pretty sure Shorty would be amazed that he mattered as much to you as anyone else.

And, of course, the reason that some Shorty's don't know how much you care is because we've all learned that there has to be one Shorty in the crowd so the rest of us can feel better about ourselves.

Now, don't get me wrong. I love nicknames. I grew up in a family full of them. I suspect you have a special name for each us, and in fact that name is the same: Mine.

Dear God:
Does Steve Spurrier annoy you?

If he doesn't, that proves you are God, and the rest of us, outside of that band of heretics known as Gator fans, are mere mortals.

Prior to his arrival, the Gators were talent rich, booster rich, and lost more than they should given those two important college football criteria. And then he showed up, and I've found new ways to dislike the Gainesville entry into the SEC.

It's not just that he wins; it's the way he wins. I'm not talking about the Fun and Gun or the trick plays or the parade of All-Americans who perpetually show up on the roster. I'm talking about him. He annoys me. You know why? It's his attitude. As my wife correctly summarized when she sat down and watched him for a few minutes, it's because his face is so expressive. Let me translate: He's smug.

What gives him the right to win with that attitude? What gives him the right to change quarterbacks on every play just to suit his whim? Of course, we all know he's actually the quarterback and the rest of these guys are plug-ins since he's run out of eligibility. He's resorted to recruiting quarterbacks from Canada. Talk about adding insult to injury.

Here's something to think about. Do you wear a headset? We talk about talking to you a lot when we're in religious circles, and we often use your name in a variety of colorful variations when we're angry or amazed. Do you have your own headset to hear our declarations? When we ask you for a corner blitz on our nasty boss, are you standing over on the sideline, so to speak, in a headset? Or do you just snatch it from one of your associates when you want to call your own play and need a little input from the other end of the line?

And though a headset is unlikely, a visor seems, well, sort of ridiculous for you. But, if you did wear one, would you turn it sideways on your head, throw it, or talk out of the side of your mouth when the play you call isn't executed as planned? After all, you could have run the play better than anybody on the field, sort of like Steve. And aside from that noted show of criticism when you benched the people of Israel for an additional forty years, have you openly said "our offense stinks" during a halftime interview?

It appears to me that sometimes Steve thinks he's you. But you don't do that kind of stuff, do you?

You'd have to be annoyed with Steve Spurrier. You are, aren't you?

There is one thing I must confess. I remember when Spurrier stopped at Duke for a couple cups of coffee. I remember watching the tube one rainy day when his Blue Devils wore out the local crew from down the road here, and I was greatly pleased. I even remember thinking what a great coach this guy was.

So, is my problem Spurrier or Spurrier's employer? To be more specific, was it easier to overlook Spurrier's smugness when he was on the side that didn't threaten my side? He *has* publicly disdained opponents on the schedule that he didn't think were worthy, which leads to the question of why he was playing them in the first place. Vince Dooley could make the Northeastern School of Polymers look like Alabama in '92, and that's what coaches are supposed to do, isn't it?

Is Steve Spurrier the perfect example of someone I'd admire if he were doing *me* some favors? Is he that successful guy who we all want to be associated with until he streaks past us into daily immortality?

Let me clarify. I'm not talking about the guy who made his way up the corporate ladder by dressing for success or by learning a lexicon of buzz words or by showing an ongoing aggressive streak to prove he had fire in his belly when the rest of us knew he was dumb as a stump. I'm talking about someone who is quite smart and shows it in a very demonstrative way.

That's Spurrier. At least I think it is. Truth is, I've never met Steve Spurrier. Truth is, I'll likely never meet him. Truth is, I'd like to, and I can honestly say it's not because it would make for good story-telling fodder. I'd like to meet him to see what he's really like.

I might find that he's what I thought he was, an insufferable, arrogant jerk. Or, I might find he's a decent, honorable guy who loves to win and doesn't much care for pretending otherwise. Truth is, I'd prefer the former over the latter. It makes him so much easier to dislike when he's wreaking havoc on my football loyalties.

I must admit that I saw a different side of Mr. Spurrier when his lads were getting whipped soundly by Alabama in the S.E.C. Championship Game. I thought he looked properly humbled. You had the Bear in on that one didn't you?

Seriously, I saw someone who hurts as much as any of the rest of us. He can't hide *that* either, even when he's squatting down examining the artificial turf and Camera 4 can't capture every facial tic.

So, how do you want me to view this guy? How do you want me to treat this familiar stranger? Jesus said the two greatest commandments were to love you with all of our being and to love our neighbor just as much as we love ourselves. It's been pointed out numerous times that, to love your neighbor or your wife or your children, you must possess a healthy love for yourself. Today we call that "self-esteem".

Self-esteem is that thing Spurrier possesses in high levels. I suppose a case could be made that lack of self-esteem is a primary cause for dislike of Spurrier's apparent high level of self-esteem. It's hard to like a winner when you don't feel like one yourself unless he's winning on your behalf.

To take this analysis one step further, I'd have to admit that the combination of genetics and upbringing that created me has to be balanced against the fact that you love someone as loveable as me and Steve Spurrier equally. In light of that one essential truth, we're all worthy of loving and being loved, no matter where our football loyalties lie.

I just hope you aren't asking me to kiss and make-up with Steve Spurrier.

Dear God:
Do you know where I can get
a good deal on stained glass?

My wife has decided she likes stained glass. Frankly, I hadn't given it much thought until it became a gift item. So now on Christmas, birthdays, and anniversaries, I know the stained glass option is valid, at least until she has every glass surface of the house covered.

Admittedly, I haven't sprung for the real stuff yet. I've only ventured into the "suncatcher" variety, which I'm pretty sure is acrylic or a polymeric variation. But, like most works of art, it takes someone far more discerning than I am to tell the difference. If I'm going to buy the real stuff, I need a deal. Can you help me out?

The other thing I'd like to know is why it's called stained. I understand the process by which stained glass is made is akin to staining, but there must have been plenty of other things to call it: kaleidoscopic glass, or multi-colored refractional glass, or Epic Images of Supreme Majesty glass. Maybe stained isn't so bad.

Isn't it odd how we come up with a name for an item, a name that represents the item's basic purpose or historical roots, and then the story behind the naming becomes secondary to the image the name comes to represent? Somewhere deep in the roots of any name lies the basicness of its creation, yet the application of that name draws a much deeper image that leaves the original name foundering in the dusts of its beginnings.

Take for example, depression glass. From a quick trip on the Internet, I learned it was a low-cost glass made during the Great Depression. All I knew about it prior to that quick reference check was that I'd seen it in stores, it wasn't cheap, and it appeared to be created with intentional imperfections blown into it. There must be a great human analogy somewhere in that idea.

Anyway, depression glass was like the occasional dish premiums offered by grocery stores. People could buy it cheap, a nickel in some cases for a saucer or a plate. As you know, my parents spent the formative years of their lives during the Great Depression. I suspect they were less concerned about the plate than about what was going on the plate. Of course, from that experience, they also learned to be savers instead of consumers and until recently to vote primarily for the party that was good enough for Roosevelt. I wonder how many of the people who grew up in the Great Depression find depression glass romantic today?

When I see depression glass in an antique store, I don't think about the hardships people endured. I don't consider that the Great Depression started with a vision of endless prosperity and the greed that vision eventually brings. Nor, do I consider the people who bet all their chips, and a few they didn't have, in the power of the stock market, leaving more than a few to cash their chips in for good when the market crashed. I don't see any of those things. I see a price tag.

Today, real depression glass or faux depression glass is a sought-after treasure used for home decor as a means of looking different from others, those who have non-depressed glass I suppose. We'll keep buying it until a majority of fashion-conscious folks have some depression glass somewhere in their house. Talk about going back to your roots.

But what I'm really after is the stained-glass angle. When did you put your official seal of approval on stained glass as the glass medium by which you could be identified? Since it happened well before the advent of licensing agreements, I assume this was a grassroots movement you let gain ground on its own. In our modern world, you'd have carefully considered proposals from three or four stained-glass producers before making a decision. There's a lot of money to be made from licensing. Not that you really need the money, but as the writer of Proverbs should have said, "You can't be too rich or too thin."

Since I started thinking about stained glass, I've been paying attention to the particular stained glass in Your House, which is what we call a church building. You know, the building with the steeple where some of us get together on a weekly basis to worship you. The stained glass in this version of Your House doesn't have any images. There's no birth, no miracles (particularly the water to wine one in a Baptist church building), no Temptations (or Supremes for that matter), no crucifixion and no resurrection. Our stained glass is multiple shades of yellows and oranges and blues. It's quite nice.

But I noted a couple of things about our stained glass. Its opacity lets in soft, beautiful light. Yet, it's impossible to actually see outside. Now, I've passed on a couple of good analogies on the depression glass angle, but I'll try a few out here.

Is stained glass a little like most of our relationships with you? You can and do shine your light in and illuminate our souls. At its very received best, that light is soft and peaceful and diffuse with all the colors of your nature. We often have trouble letting that light out clearly to the people around us. Instead of shining with softness and peace and color, it comes out dull and clouded.

Why is that? Is it because only you can shine the type of light that makes stained glass uniquely beautiful, or is it because our internal light projectors are often clogged with guilt and doubt and envy and all manner of things that don't represent your nature? I could use a good cleaning. I don't project you nearly as well as you've projected into me.

Another analogy I'd like to try out on you is the idea that stained glass is a lot like some churches: the effect inside is much nicer than the effect outside.

Perhaps, since I'm waxing analogous with you, I can try one

more. If we can't see out, we don't have to acknowledge that Your World is a lot bigger than the four walls of Your House. Could it be that if we had less stained glass, we'd have greater vision for Your World (as well as quite a few less analogies)?

Please let me know. I'm having trouble seeing some things clearly right now.

Dear God:
Have you ever watched
Celebrity Skiing?

As you know, my son received a five-inch television for Christmas from a well-meaning relative. Now that he can take it with him on all car trips over five minutes, I've learned many of the fascinating things we can watch on the five or six non-cable-dependent channels in this market.

One of the finer offerings on Christmas Day was *Celebrity Skiing*. Now, I recognized Robbie Knievel, but the celebrity Franco Gibatterando, or something like that, didn't register with me. Nonetheless, these two celebrities were racing each other through a course at some ski resort. I'm not sure of the prizes awarded to the winners. In fact, I'm not sure of much about this event because, as soon as I heard Celebrity Skiing and those two names, I took a York Peppermint Pattie break in my head and went to a far-away land as I drove along.

All I'm sure of is that two people who made a name for themselves doing something besides skiing were on television Christmas Day skiing in front of a national audience that must have numbered at least into the hundred of thousands, maybe into the millions. Why would people take a perfectly good holiday and spend it glued to the tube watching two amateur skiers race each other down a mountain in some ski resort they'll never see? Why would these hundreds of thousands or possibly million-plus people invest time watching that event on a day that is still marginally about the birth of your son and has some semblance of family tied to it? Other than the oxygen deprivation that affects the brain after a big Christmas dinner, I can't imagine what the attraction might be.

Now, if the race had been on local television and featured Hank from the cable company and Luther from Sears racing wild boars down Main Street, I might see the draw. At a minimum, Hank's and Luther's families would certainly want to tune in for this auspicious moment as would their coworkers and neighbors. I'm sure the wild-boar lovers of the area would also watch. I understand that. Those folks at least have some relevance to the viewers' lives. We at least know the Luther's and Hank's of this world.

Is the lure of celebrity, real or conjured, more interesting to viewers than finding out if Hank and Luther are accomplished *boarquestrians?* I would think the drama of wondering if Hank, for example, has enough insurance to cover the costs of raising four children if he meets an untimely end is at least as dramatic as wondering if Robbie will hit the last gate on the way down.

Did Luther, in fact, receive a DieHard® battery sponsorship from Sears based on the huge battery embroidered onto the back of his shirt? Hank and Luther and the ebb and flow of their daily lives are as real as it gets. As best I can tell, celebrities live on another plane, or another planet, because none of them show up at any of the places I go every day.

Begin the title of a televised program with the word celebrity, and viewership of at least moderate amounts is guaranteed, no matter if the event would have any interest for the viewer otherwise. It could have been Celebrity Pie Baking, Celebrity Speed Walking, or Celebrity Celery Eating.

Does our preference for anything vaguely related to celebrity bother you? It has been said more than once lately that celebrity has become the new religion. I can't say I disagree. And I might even understand why. It has to do with our priorities. No, wait. It has more to do with how unfulfilling we find our daily lives so we look to images of fame to dream of how it might be were we in their shoes; or something like that.

A copy of *People* has once again made its way into our house. You know the one: "The Twenty-Five Most Intriguing People" issue. I caught the cover and noted that all of the photos are of people who are readily recognizable without having their names captioned, though *People* does go to that trouble in case a reader just emerged from living in a cave for the last five years.

I'd much rather read about the guy who hangs out on the boulevard with the Scottish Kilt, the sash, the medals, and the sandwich board proclaiming something or the other as I drive by at fifty miles per hour. That's intriguing. But you'll never see him in *People* though you'll see Prince Charles and his bony legs fishing up a storm in his kilt.

I'd like to see a story about someone who defied all the odds to raise twenty-five orphans in a three-bedroom house or someone who refused to leave a decaying neighborhood to bring it back to life. Of course, that kind of story only occasionally makes it into *People*. Those stories are more of a *Readers Digest* saga, which isn't nearly glossy enough for the folks who buy *People*. *People* would run an article about whether the twenty-five orphans in the house were wearing Hilfiger or Polo hand-me-downs.

My son just came in to inform me that there are only about 450 cheetahs left in Africa. If I were a celebrity, would the nanny have already put him to bed?

Your answer to celebrity is quite clear in the gospels. You remember the rich, young ruler who came to Jesus and asked what he must do to be a follower. Jesus told him to divest (now there's a modern word thrown into an old story) of all his holdings and follow him. As you'll remember from this event, the rich, young ruler couldn't part with all he had, for he had much, and went away. Does celebrity have that effect on all of us? Do we recognize that there is more in life than celebrity and wealth, yet parting with our fondness for those things is too difficult a change to make?

Perhaps you sent Jesus at the point in history that you did because of the lack of tabloid press that existed in those days. You've always been a grassroots sort of God. You prefer to build one person at a time rather than to sweep the fancy of millions by a well-placed interview or profile.

How would Jesus be treated in our world today? A few decades ago, he would probably have been declared a dangerous radical, particularly by Your Church. Today, he would have his moment of celebrity until we rushed on to the next thing which titillated our imaginations.

This is a very strange world of yours we're living in today. The more bizarre the behavior, the more famous one becomes. I'd like to think that, if you sent Jesus around today, you would do so without his having an agent or a publicity tour. I can't see him at a book signing or the opening of a car dealership. And I certainly can't see him dressing as a bride for his own wedding, but times change.

I suspect we'd see him, instead, at the three-bedroom house where the orphans are being raised or in the declining neighborhood replacing some plumbing. I recollect my favorite passage from the Bible, the one that deals with the sheep and the goats. You know, the story Jesus told his followers: "When did we visit you in prison, clothe you when you were naked, feed you when you were hungry?" Of course, the response from Jesus was and is today, "whenever you did it to the least of my (people), you did it to me."

Perhaps, I need to realize that each of us is a celebrity in your eyes, marked for the most special attention any of us can receive. Just help me remember that the next time I cast a lustful eye at the attention some guys receive skiing on Christmas Day.

Dear God:
Did you store any water for Y2K?

I know you don't actually need water, or ice for that matter. You don't actually need anything but us, apparently. That's the only reason you've stuck around this long, isn't it?

Now that the first Y2K milestone is past, all of us are breathing a sigh of relief. I imagine you've had a good grin or two at some of our follies. It's amazing how many people made presentations at conferences, how many company meetings were held, how many barbershop discussions centered around a topic such as the Y2K bug, and how many churches held worship services dealing with the damage we've done to ourselves. Our manmade follies ought to be pretty self-evident to the dullest of your flock, shouldn't it?

It isn't that I don't think Y2K was a serious event, but I can't imagine that more than one-tenth of one-tenth of one percent of the world's population, or maybe even the computer programming population, understood the specifics of what might happen.

Let me see if I can get this whole business marginally straight. At the stroke of midnight January 1, 2000, or on the 2000 leap year, which is the extra day we throw in every four years to make up for that annoying quarter day you stuck in the earth's orbit around the sun, a computer can't figure out what day it is and ceases to function. If that computer happens to be controlling the systems that keep the nuclear fuel rods submerged in whatever they're submerged in, then the nuclear plant could experience a melt-down, and we'd all be with you sooner than expected. Is that right? Sort of?

There's a missing ingredient here, I think. Aside from running some simulations to see how systems would react, we didn't actually know for certain what would happen. We spent much money and time on the fixes and seem, after a few days into the new year, to have done it right. Did we?

Here's what I don't understand. When this problem first began to gain widespread attention, there was a quick shift to the worst-case scenario by a lot of people, many of whom speak regularly on Your Behalf. I had the honor of attending one such session, which was dressed up as something else, but that's another story.

The speaker began by stating that we might get to January 2 or so and have nothing happen. Then, he disregarded his qualifying statement and began to tell the audience, which appeared to be made up of business types and such, all the horrific things that could happen. He claimed to have spent 2,000 hours on research of this millennial phenomenon (ironic, don't you think?) and went into great depth about the use of satellites which track the trains which carry the food which winds up on our supermarket shelves which we buy and digest for our daily bread. Somehow, this whole system had a pretty good chance of crashing and sending people into the streets to loot and pillage, which used to be a fine American tradition in less-settled times.

He also explored the calamity that came out of a power outage in some major American city in the last few years and went into graphic detail about what happens in a high-rise building when the plumbing stops working. Not that any of this would happen, mind you, but that it darn well could.

The whole point of this exercise was to let the attendees know that Y2K was essentially going to be the opportunity for people to come back to you. He made an eloquent case about declining moral standards in our country which, on the whole, I found accurate. He also drew from some Old Testament scripture, which escapes me now although I know it was one of the minor prophets who lived in a comparably sinful time to ours and prophesied of your judgment.

I have to ask you while we're on the topic if you considered prophets minor or major, and, if the moral climate during periods of Old Testament history was as bad as today. I think I know the answer to the former (no distinction in your eyes), but the latter is probably what I'm writing to you about today—at least part of what I'm writing about. I'll come back to that question.

The first thing I really wanted to know (and I am thankful you're patient) is why some people of faith seem to rush to worst-case scenarios more quickly than the rest of the population. I think I know part of the answer, which I'll try out on you, but I hope you'll help me see the whole answer as you think fitting for my mental and/or spiritual capacity. I think the first part of the answer has to do with how some people view you. I think that some people of faith virtually see you as their possession and that, in that role, anyone who doesn't agree with them should be first in line for your judgment.

I sensed from listening to this gentlemen speak that he wanted something to happen (which he'd deny if asked of course), just to prove that he'd been right all along and so that people would be forced to repent and come back to you on the merits of his moral stewardship. As believers, we sometimes tend to feel we have the moral high ground on the rest of the world, and anything bad that happens to them is richly deserved. Of course, the Bible teaches that we're all sinners, but we like to measure things in degrees of sin though you've rarely drawn that distinction.

Speaking of the Bible, I once read a book by one of your wisest contemporary authors who detailed the sweep of history in the Old Testament. You created the world and man. Man rebelled. You picked individuals like Joseph and Moses to do great things on your behalf, very ordinary people I might add. People stuck with them as long as times were good. You paved the way for a young boy named David to be an earthly king of your people. He was a powerful ruler until power corrupted him. You moved on to prophets to battle the political establishment. Time after time after time you took a wayward, unfocused people back into your arms when they repented.

And then one day, you said, "Enough." The result was the man of your own seed named Jesus. During and after the recounting of Jesus' life, death, and resurrection, the tenor of the Bible changes. It changes from the dark heaviness of the Old Testament to hope, love, and forgiveness.

Why do we still want to be prophets of doom when you've given us the tools to bring light to the entire world? Maybe we're like the people of Israel in the Old Testament. We don't learn very well from history. Or maybe we just haven't learned yet that the all-consuming love you showed through Jesus is a better way to reach your world.

Now, God, if I said these things to many of my friends they'd say that I was soft on crime and a bleeding-heart liberal to boot. If I said these things to some of my most religious friends, they'd further say that I'm discounting your judgment. I'm not.

I just can't see that any of us have the wisdom to project what you're planning to do which, in fact, you've confirmed in the Bible. I guess we don't read that part very often. Does this sound a little like our preparation for Y2K? We're not sure what's going to happen, but let's all expect the worst.

Back to the other question: Are these the worst of times in your eyes? People have been preaching Jesus' return for a long time now, and it seems that tragedy after disaster after moral outrage keeps piling up around us. We're going through a period right now when many of us have decided we have personal rights that allow us to do what we want, no matter what the effect to ourselves or others might be.

You've taken a pretty good beating in some quarters here because of this new moral climate, but is it any worse by degree than the people of Israel's worshipping a golden calf in the desert while Moses was meeting with you? I'd hate to have been caught red-handed on that one!

Perhaps the most negative attitude I see going on around me today is fear. As you know, four boys, including my son, spent the night here New Year's Eve. As the Times Square ball came down and the power stayed on, one of them began to shout, "We're still alive! we're still alive!" He did this in a joking manner, but I think I sensed some palpable relief in all their expressions.

Are we like those boys? Do we claim faith while our hearts flutter? Jesus said to his disciples, "Don't be afraid." I also remember the passage of scripture that says, "Perfect love casts out fear." Is there any love more perfect than yours? I'd have to say "No" so perhaps the ingredient we're missing most is your deeply felt love in how we view the world around us.

God, would you help me not to be afraid? Would you do the same for others? I can't help but think that, if we were less afraid, people would see your hand at work more than they do now, and perhaps we wouldn't be so ready to listen every time someone comes up with a new way you're going to even the score.

By the way, did I tell you the speaker had also written a book on the subject?

34

Dear God:
Were you for the North or the
South during the Civil War?

After all, we were all your people. My ancestors, Southerners, claimed you as did all those people from up North. You know who I'm talking about—the people who used to come down here and leave their money during vacation but are now in the process of taking over again.

As you know, this particular subject is a sore spot of mine. I'm very proud of being a Southerner. I've always taken great pride in the manners we were taught, the general bent toward treating people with respect, speaking to people you don't know and will never see again, offering directions when you're in line at a convenience store even though you weren't asked—that kind of thing. Frankly, I'd trust a good old redneck any day of the week over a fast-talking Yankee. I've come to learn of late that choosing sides isn't quite that simple any more.

Somewhere back in my ancestral history, I'm pretty sure the folks who eventually led to my being here were on the Southern side of the Civil War. I don't know if any of them fought or what their stories might have been. With one possible exception, I'm pretty sure none of them owned slaves. If they did, any wealth they might have accumulated through such status went away long before my parents or grandparents were brought into this world.

The point is that I came from ordinary stock, which I'm quite proud of as you know. Knowing the emotional tendencies I've inherited, my ancestors felt quite sure you were on their side, whether they were right or wrong, which still isn't far from where any of us from the South, North, East or West are today.

I'm not trying to ask you whether you take sides in a war or not. That question is far too complex an issue for me, but I am wondering how the same types of issues that brought us into a bloody, non-productive conflict can still have such an emotional effect on us today.

As far as I know, there aren't any people around who were in the Civil War. You wouldn't know that fact to hear some of us talk. One thing about Southerners is that we have our pride in large measure. I wonder if that pride doesn't come from the fact that we suffered so much for so long after fighting a losing battle.

You know what I'm trying to get around to saying, but I've been attempting to lay a little groundwork for my own benefit. Today happens to be the day our blessed nation celebrates Martin Luther King's Birthday. As you know, in my equally blessed state of South Carolina, we don't cotton to the idea of Martin Luther King's Birthday as a state holiday. We're like the old cigarette commercial; We'd rather fight than switch, and like the cigarette commercial, we've got the black eyes to prove it.

As you'll recollect, South Carolinians have been fighting the Civil War a long time, in fact, since we started it. Though no one here today took part in the carnage, most of us still take pride in firing the first shots of the Civil War. I know it's foolish to take pride in an act that didn't do anybody a bit of good unless, of course, someone descended from a slave or a carpetbagger. Yet, there's something to be said for any event that brings recognition to our beautiful but small state even if it's a war which put most people in near ruinous poverty for many years.

That's my problem. While the rest of the world has moved on, we still feel the need to let everybody know we started the Civil War and to use the Confederate battle flag as a sign of defiance. Now, I've gotten around to it.

There was supposed to be a big march in Columbia today by folks who want the Confederate battle flag removed from the top of the state house. I haven't bothered to check the news to see how many showed up, how many of them were black, how many of them were white, and, most importantly, how many of them were from out of state. When it comes down to it, we're less interested in what black folk in the state might do as to what those agitators from outside the state might be planning. I have to admit, and you know what's in my heart that I'm also in that camp. I don't want people—black, white or of the Yankee persuasion in particular—coming here and telling any of us what to do.

I just wish some of us had more sense. One camp claims the Confederate battle flag flying over the state house is a symbol of our heritage to which they've added, "not hate." The other contingent, mostly composed of black folk, see the flag as a sign of slavery and all the evil deeds perpetrated in the name of keeping white folk on top and black folk where they belong.

I'm more than a little tired of both camps. The way I see it, the idea behind the Confederacy has been dead since New England textile mill owners began coming to our state and hiring my ancestors for next to slave wages. Those folks from the North came as close to slavery without actually owning someone as has been seen in this country since, well, since people in the Northeast and West and other places began paying Asian immigrants slave wages to produce clothing.

If we have some resentment to vent, it ought to be directed toward the people who took advantage of our situation when we couldn't help ourselves. But, you know a little history, and you know that sort of thing has been going on a long time and will continue as long as there's somebody out there who can be taken advantage of and somebody else who doesn't mind taking advantage.

At the same time, black folk have come a long way. I understand there's deep-seeded prejudice about the black community. It has been a hard row to hoe, and they haven't acquired anywhere near equality yet. I'll admit I carry my own stereotypes around though I'm not proud of a single one of them. I have a growing problem with folks who cry foul anytime anything doesn't go their way, and who know the collective guilt we all feel will ultimately be enough of a lever to get things changed. Of course, I haven't walked a mile, or even three feet in their shoes, so maybe I'm wrong.

I'm pretty sure that I'm not wrong that the majority of the people of this state wouldn't be so upset about the matter if it weren't for two percent of the population on both sides stirring up the dust of emotions as best they can. I wish we put less stock in symbols and more stock in living productive lives. I'd bet that before the flag became an issue, most people who visited or drove by the state house didn't note which flags were flying over the top unless they were so instructed, either as an insult or a matter of pride. Perhaps you could remove the state house through some non-fatal act, and then we could go back to living lives that aren't driven by a piece of fabric.

This whole nasty affair is a tug-of-war between white folk who don't want to give in any more to black folk and black folk who want to see how far they can push this issue. That's the whole commotion in a nutshell. It's not about heritage; it's not about a symbol of hatred. It's about two irresistible forces meeting two immovable objects; it's about defining who has power.

The black folk are going to win in the end because the Confederate battle flag flying over the state house is about as appropriate as my flying the British Union Jack in front of my house. It's a sad thing to watch no matter which side you might be naturally drawn to, which is a proper Southern way of using a preposition to end a phrase, black or white.

There's a bigger issue here. Many of the folks on both sides of the issue claim you as their ruling authority. In fact, there are more than a couple of preacher types in both camps. Is that what you intended? When I look back at Jesus' life, he had the ultimate authority over life and death and chose death as a recourse to showing how much power he had, simply for the purpose of proving how much you loved all of us. All I'm seeing right now are people staking out turf.

I'm also reminded that we're all slaves to sin, whether we like to use that term anymore or not, and that, in your eyes, the biggest thing we need to take down are the veneers of respectability most of us try to put over ourselves when we leave the house every morning.

I hope you'll help us see the light. I hope, in the end, you'll put enough good sense into the heads of people in power on both sides of the coin to see how destructive this whole issue is, and that when we all learn to be servants of each other, there's no telling what you might accomplish in this great state of ours.

Note: In 2000, legislation was passed and enacted to remove the Confederate battle flag from the state house dome and place it on the grounds of the state house. The legislation included establishment of Martin Luther King's Birthday and Confederate Memorial Day as official state holidays. This compromise relieved the "flag fatigue" most of the state was feeling but failed to relieve the anger of those on the extremes of each side of the issue.

Dear God:
Will we need SUV's in Heaven?

I suppose this question begs several other such questions as, "Does it snow in heaven?" and "How do people get around up there?" That's not what I'm after. Since the only way I can relate to you is through earthly conditions, I'd like to know how you view this SUV phenomenon we're experiencing. If you do have a stable of cars, is one of them an SUV for trips to the store, bank, school, and all those other things I have to associate with heaven to have any comprehension at all?

Otherwise, heaven is a place where people sit around on their celestial front porch and wave to their neighbors as they walk by. Of course, if it snows in heaven, front porches won't hold quite the charm I might imagine. But if it's 72° with 15 percent humidity all the time, front porches may in fact, be a highlight of every home. As you can tell, I have many questions about heaven and none about its opposite, but let's revisit that another time. There are a few things I'd like to do here, even given the climatic hazards and having to work for a living.

What I'd really like to know is how you view this SUV craze. As you know, we had a bit of snow over the weekend, enough for a Minnesotan to put on a very light sweater and enough for a South Carolinian to break into a cold, panic-driven sweat. You'll remember I was out and about Saturday night doing the normal errands to the grocery store, to Blockbuster, and to other places.

I was in a car, a Japanese car. I'm not sure how much it snows in Japan. In my driving near the neighborhood, I noticed three cars abandoned, two of which were in ditches. Of these cars, two were SUV's and one was a Volvo, which is from Sweden where it snows a great deal. But you already know that.

I was struck by the amusing irony that three cars engineered for adverse conditions met their match under our one-inch barrage of frozen precipitation, but it reminded me that all the precautions built into these fine and equally expensive vehicles are subject to the skill of the driver involved. I imagine you could take the aforementioned Minnesotan and put him in a '73 Dodge Dart with bald tires and a slipping transmission who could whistle some song of the North in any key requested while cruising the streets.

Are SUV's sought for their tank-like safety features rather than their four-wheel drive capability? If so, why do the automakers keep making them with four-wheel drive? Actually, I know the answer to that question. The automakers keep making them with four-wheel drive because those models cost more and sell better. That fact still doesn't explain why the consuming public keeps demanding four-wheel drive, at least in this part of the world. Unless, of course, there are plenty of families who go out four-wheeling on the weekends.

The fact is that people buy four-wheel drive vehicles because it sounds like a great idea. They have notions that these expensive pieces of machinery are, in fact, a guarantee of safety, particularly when the unfortunate driver of the other car is behind the wheel of a sub-compact. There's the prestige angle as well, and let's not forget the ability to put the family lab into one of these vehicles so that it can stink up the nice leather seats.

Ah, you know where I'm heading with this one. It has to do with our bent toward protecting ourselves from the slings and arrows of modern life by encasing ourselves in all sorts of armor: SUV's, security systems, cell phones, GPS locators, neighborhood security; the list goes on and on. You know I've fallen prey to many of these things. It's a dangerous world we live in. Ask anyone who shows up on the victim side of an accident or a crime blotter. I wonder if we haven't turned our trust in you over to a variety of gizmos designed to protect us from ourselves.

I'll admit it. Bad things in my life have typically happened as a result of me doing some completely stupid act that left me wondering after the fact what, if anything, I must have been thinking. I know there are a lot of people who never did anything to deserve the bad that came their way.

Where am I to look for protection from life's mishaps when I don't deserve them? I could look to you, but are you going to stop the idiots I see run traffic lights everyday without a thought for anyone else? Are you going to protect me from people who change lanes on the interstate five times in a quarter of a mile when we're all driving well past the posted speed limit? There are people who think you'll protect them if they walk across a six-lane highway without checking traffic in either direction before starting. I haven't heard from any of them lately.

Or, in fact, do you protect us in small but significant ways every day? Are you there when we almost pull out in front of one of the red-light runners but were reaching for the tape that fell to the floorboard when we stopped for the light? Is it you who helps us decide to take the back road home, narrowly missing the ten-car pile-up on the interstate or that leads us onto the interstate when the normal back roads home had a tragedy of their own?

It might be that none of those questions are fair. Perhaps the bigger question is what exactly you want us to seek out of our relationship to you. I can't help but think after four decades of life that it isn't the traffic accidents we have or avoid, but the way we go out the door approaching life every morning that's more a reflection of your influence in our lives than any negative event that does or doesn't happen to us.

I've never been able to reconcile the view of more than a few that you're like some big bodyguard who keeps us safe. The problem with that view is that, when a tragedy occurs we expected you to prevent, we tend to believe that you either deserted us or that we deserved our bad fortune.

I've already leveled with you about the lack of good sense I've shown at times in my life and the bad results that came out of those mental leaves of absence. Where are you when something bad happens out of the blue that we did absolutely nothing more than get out of bed that morning to deserve? You're not playing bodyguard at that point, are you?

Or are you? Is your style of bodyguarding more concerned with our ongoing relationship with you? Man has survived all of history by going through accidents, plagues, droughts, floods, and inhumane treatment at the hands of bad people, and still found you in the moments of terror *and* peace.

In fact, it seems the people who have survived to earn admiration in the chronicles of history, including the Bible, were people who overcame adversity that came their way without reason. In another corner, we've also come to admire people who fell flat on their face in the area of sin but turned around and did great deeds. You are the God of second chances, are you not?

Let's get back to this SUV discussion. Before I went down the other path, I was simply trying to make the connection between the material symbols that hold such magic for us and how we might view our relationships with you today. I'm not trying to insult people who have nice vehicles. I'm just wondering if perhaps we haven't decided that the abundant life you promised is just fine as long we can establish our own qualifications for where it fits into our life styles.

As most people, I have dreamed of being rich enough to buy what I want, do what I want, and generally thumb my nose at the rest of the world if I feel like it, but I know from studying your nature and seeing people who truly live at peace with themselves *and* you that the answer has a lot more to do with having a vision for a world cut from your cloth, a cloth that is simple but well-tailored to a person's talents. We're all prone to speak sentiments like: "as long as you have your health" and "there's no blessing like children" as long as we're not looking at what the neighbors just parked in their driveway.

Help me to see the world with the balance you possess, a balance that makes me want to excel in my work, give back to my community, love unlovable people in your name, and be satisfied with what I have when I know it's enough, whether other people less deserving than me have more or not.

At the same time, help me to feel confident that you protect me in all sorts of ways every day in a manner I might not ever understand.

One other thing; The next time it snows, help me to pay attention to the roads and not to lose control as I laugh at someone's SUV that landed in a ditch.

Dear God: If you were a car dealer, how would your commercials sound?

I was driving somewhere yesterday and heard a commercial for a car dealership in our area. The commercial went on at length about the dealer's commitment to understanding the customer's needs, treating the customer with respect, and then letting nature take its course. The part about letting nature take its course wasn't specifically what he said, but that's what he implied.

He implied the customer would naturally buy from his firm because of the dealer's attention to the customer's needs and his commitment to treating the customer with respect. Of course, at the end of the commercial, he couldn't help himself and went on to say that, if you found a better deal anywhere else, his dealership would beat it. Bring in a newspaper ad, get a quote off the Internet, send an offer by carrier pigeon, wheel your 90-year-old grandmother in with a price—he'd beat it.

Am I missing something here? What I think I'm hearing is someone's looking for respect. Car dealers, in particular, have been maligned by their customers for years for the methods they've used to cajole people to buy cars. If buying a car weren't the second biggest investment most of us make, we'd treat their antics much the same as we do a carnival huckster. Except for the most naïve among us, the carnival huckster's not going to empty our pockets in nearly as significant a way as the car dealer.

47

I've been around long enough to know the car dealer world has all kinds of consultants. There are consultants who tell dealers how to arrange the cars on the lot for the maximum impact. There are consultants who specialize in signage and color schemes and the number of potted plants to put inside the showroom and the perfect location of those plants.

There are consultants who are now telling car dealers about relationships. These consultants and the car dealers who do a little business reading on the side know we're going through a phase in the business world where the emphasis is on building relationships with customers. No matter what anyone says, it has become darn hard to compete on price alone.

We call this concept the relational approach versus the transactional approach to business. The idea is that if you build a solid relationship with a prospective or repeat customer, the customer will overcome pricing differences, criminal background checks, and a host of other obstacles to buy from you because they like you—*just* because they like you; in other words, they trust you.

In this particular case, I heard a car dealer telling people, "I want you to trust me. I care about the type of car you actually need, not the most expensive one I can sell you. I'll tell you which options are bad deals and help you make good decisions based on value. I won't exaggerate the performance of the car. When I tell you our service department is a caring, efficient organization of professionals, you can take my word for it."

Then, I heard him say, "But if you don't believe me, we'll still beat anybody's price." I'll bet unsaid among those who actually bothered to listen to the commercial many were thinking, "Yeah, but what's that price based on? Who gets the rebate? Where are the hidden charges?" So much for trust.

Of course, there's "the screamer." "Drive it, push it, tow it, or have it dropped from a helicopter on to our lot. We'll give you top trade dollar." The best I can say for him up front is that I know he's been honest enough through his schtick to let me know he plans to stick it to me if he gets the chance.

There's the volume dealer. You know I travel around the state a bit. Did you know there are several dealers in several cities who sell more cars of their make than anyone else in the state? I'm not very astute with numbers, but I do know that statistics can tell almost any tale you'd like to tell if the numbers are presented the right way.

The idea behind this approach is that, if these dealers are selling more cars than anyone else, there must be a good reason to buy from them. That's the kind of guy I run from because if everyone else is doing it, there must be something wrong with it.

With the snow last week, a few dealers have whipped out the "inventories piling up because of the massive snow storm, we're giving 'em away just to get 'em off the lot" approach. No doubt the snow storm didn't make people think about driving a new car, and folks certainly weren't out in force kicking the tires when there was an inch of ice underfoot.

In my naïve way, wouldn't the folks who were in the market for a new car be back the next week anyway? Do automakers give big rebates because there was snow in five percent of their market area? If they don't, who's going to pay in the end?

Back to my original question. If you were a car dealer, how would your commercials sound? I suppose for a quick answer I'd go back to the original example: build relationships; real relationships that show people how much you care. Demonstrate your caring to the community by finding transportation for the less fortunate among us. Be out there; be involved. Then, let nature take its course.

How would you advertise? If I could be your ad agency for a minute, I'd like to suggest a novel approach. Instead of trying to lure people in with the idea of great deals, you would take the high road:

> "Hi, this is God. I've just opened a dealership out on the Motor Mile. I have cars. These cars provide trans-portation. They will get you from where you are to where you need to go. They will take you on long jour-neys when you need, and they will also keep you safe and dry when you're out on the road in a storm if you follow my driving advice. Some people think the cars I have are the best cars on the road. You'll have to de-cide that for yourself. Not all of you will drive my cars. All of you could, but not all of you will.
>
> This is how I operate. You're all welcome to stop by. In fact, I encourage you to stop by. I'd like to meet you, get to know you better. After we've talked a bit, I'll be happy to give you some advice on the car that's best suited to your particular needs. If the car you have is just fine right now, I'll tell you. If you're reaching for a car that is far beyond your means, I'll tell you. Though I could work it out for you to drive that car, having a car you can't handle isn't a good idea.
>
> If you come by, I'll give you a free roadmap. I'm pretty good at sending people in the right direction. I'd like to send you in a direction that's best for you. I won't push, but sometimes I ask questions with knotty answers. I think answering those questions is important if you're going to own the right car.
>
> I'm open every day except Sunday, but you can find me even then. Hope to see you soon."

What do you think? I think it's the right message for you. The only problem I foresee is that given the number of com-mercials floating around out there making all sorts of outra-geous claims, you'd have to run quite a few spots to be heard, and people would take their time learning to trust you. If you're in business for the long run, that's the way to go.

By the way, it wouldn't hurt to offer a long-term warranty.

Dear God:
If you were In charge of the halftime show at the Super Bowl, what would you do?

The big day's tomorrow. Sunday. I hope you're ready. It seems almost everyone is. Parties are set, bets are made, plans are drawn. All eyes are on Atlanta, and for once it's not over airport delays or Lester Maddox-autographed ax handles. It's the Super Bowl; you know, the end-of-the-year championship football game with Roman numerals at the end.

They're playing it indoors this year, on a rug, in a cavernous building called the Georgia Dome. Before I go any further, could you outlaw that sort of playing surface? Though football's a violent game where the odds are 100% that someone is going to get hurt, the element of a piece of carpet, albeit specialized and padded, over a concrete slab, only magnifies the number of injuries that will occur, quite a few more than would take place on one of your better surfaces, grass.

The Super Bowl is one of the biggest days of the year for us. It brings together the key elements of our society in one big bundle: massive publicity, carefully planned event management, tons of advertising, and a wealth of entertainment. It's built around one key idea: money. There's also a football game.

The Super Bowl is like many aspects of life. We dream about the event, only to find when it finally happens the anticipation was the better part of the deal. I'm not talking about the game. It's a disappointment more often than not. I *am* talking about the buildup to the game as an event.

Somewhere along the way, we've been led to believe the Super Bowl somehow is a ticket to a better life, that in being part of the watching throng, our lives will be fuller. For many of us, it's an excuse to have a party, or party, which is a subtle but important difference. Anyway, I can't help but think that 135 million of us have bought the idea that the Super Bowl must be part of our lives, else we're missing something.

But you already know that. What I'd like to know is how you'd handle that most important part of the Super Bowl broadcast: the halftime show. Keep in mind the halftime show is geared around keeping people close to the tube so that they can see the two-million dollar ads interspersed between the show. Halftime is a great time to do something else during the course of a football game: start on tax returns, run to the store for more bean dip, or help your child with that homework assignment put off until Sunday night. But this is the Super Bowl, and the halftime show must be worthy.

There's just one problem: Historically, the Super Bowl halftime show attempts to be all things to all people and ends up missing on all counts. The show usually has some recognizable, but milktoast icon or two as the headliner. This performer is surrounded by the ubiquitous halftime marching band, or bands in the Super Bowl's case, and completed by hundreds of dancing men and women. The last element is a sign of the times because these types of shows used to include dozens of dancing women, but I don't mind if there are bunch of men out there shaking it as well. The reason I don't mind is because I'd rather watch the ice melt on the neighbor's house than watch the halftime show.

That's why I think you ought to take it over. And I have a suggestion:

Jimmy Swaggart. That's right, Jimmy Swaggart. He needs something notable to do these days, and nobody can work a crowd like Swaggart. He can play the piano. He can sing. He can weep profusely. In a fix he can have Jerry Lee Lewis come in as his special, unannounced guest. Nothing milktoast about those two. You'd have the place rocking.

Swaggart could introduce Jim Bakker to make a halftime pitch before 135 million viewers for the new stadium he's going to build at Heritage USA, the site of the 2010 Super Bowl. I heard Jim has said he wants to return to Heritage USA and resume his ministry, and he has Reggie White on his side. Anyway, the plan would be that each donor of $50,000 or more receives a ticket to the Super Bowl and a lifetime pass to the New Heritage USA. Just don't let Jim talk about time shares.

Let's do the math. The average NFL stadium today seats around 70,000, not counting luxury boxes. I'm going to guess you can get one built and equipped for about $250 million. At $50,000 a pop, taking out $490 for the complimentary Super Bowl ticket and $10 for the lifetime pass to Heritage USA, it would take 5,000 donors to build the stadium. You'd then have almost 65,000 regular seats left to sell for the Super Bowl at $500 per ticket (in today's dollars). Of course, boxes for the game would be, let's say, how about $200,000 each? You can easily fit 60 luxury boxes into a stadium. Now we're starting to talk real money.

The rest required to win the NFL's approval would come out of the Heritage USA marketing budget, which could get a once-in-a-lifetime boost to the park's image from having a Super Bowl there.

You have to be in on this gig. Think of the possibilities for generating revenue for Your Favorite Theme Park and the prestige you'd get from hosting a Super Bowl. You'd be bigger than an IPO for a dot-com company that's losing $100 million a year.

But there's more. Among the useless Super Bowl trivia I picked up this week, I learned the Super Bowl must be played indoors if the average temperature in the host city is below 50 degrees for the time of year the game is played. We're talking

Fort Mill, South Carolina, the last week of January, so there's no question the stadium has to be domed. I'm sure in the interest of protecting your interests, Jim will name the new facility after you: The God Dome.

Consider the possibilities. First, this approach to the half-time show returns the focus to you. And, it couldn't be done by two of your more effective communicators. You'd have two guys promoting you who fit in perfectly with the whole Super Bowl culture: deal-making, fast-talking sorts who could sell humility to Donald Trump. People wouldn't notice the difference. Instead of Pepsi, they'd hear God. As instructed, they'd send in massive amounts of money that would fund your new stadium, with no tax dollars required, and the Super Bowl would be played on your turf in ten years.

One word of caution when you're dealing with the NFL— They might ask you to bring Wayne Newton in to present a more diverse show. He has that Vegas persona that reminds people to bet heavily on the game; which, in turn, makes them watch all the way through; which, in turn, lets them view several hundred million dollars worth of commercials; which, in turn, allows the NFL to extract an enormous amount of money from the network that's willing to pony up these extraordinary dollars.

But, when you're in the *business* of being God, what's a little compromise? Jimmy, Jim, Wayne, and maybe even Jerry Lee. This could be your finest hour.

One other thought: You'd also have the only indoor stadium with perfect natural grass.

Dear God:
How does it feel being
your own boss?

I heard someone suggest a few years back that contemporary people don't comprehend the meaning of the title Lord since that sounds pretty feudal to us. If you were our Lord, the reasoning goes that we would be serfs or knaves or some type of underlings, creating a hierarchy that's beyond modern comprehension. We take great pride in neither being owned nor beholden to any parties outside of VISA and Master Card. It was suggested that, to help people who have never known you as Lord understand you better, it might be wise to refer to you as Chief Executive Officer or Chairman of the Board.

How do those titles sound to you? CEO of someone's life? It really doesn't have the same majesty as being referred to as Lord or Master, but it does have a certain ring to it when you put it in the context of business.

I have another question: How did the job become yours? I don't mean to offend you. I'd certainly never offend one who's the CEO of an operation as big as yours. But I can't help wondering how you came to be who you are.

Did you apply for the job? And, if so, who were the other applicants? More importantly, who did the hiring? The Bible isn't clear about this aspect of your CEOship. In fact, I can't recall the Bible's saying more than that you existed before anything else existed, end of question.

You created us with a brain that creates questions, and you gave us the choice of simply believing or choosing to question certain aspects of belief, so I'm sure I'm not the only one who wonders how you came to be in your current position. Perhaps I ought to leave out current since that has the ring of one who climbed the organizational ladder and implies an organization chart which takes this discussion a lot further than I originally intended. I do wonder about your basic nature.

None of that was the original question. I asked how it felt to be your own boss.

For starters, I'd guess it must be pretty lonely at times. I've heard it said that being President is the loneliest job on earth. Now, I'd have thought that running a research station in the Antarctic by yourself would be a pretty lonely job, but I can see where having the pressure of being responsible for the lives of billions would have its moments of loneliness as well.

Of course, while I've been taught that you created us to relieve your loneliness, I can't help but think the continual problems we bring your way must make you want to run away at times. Of course you're God, and, perhaps as the really big CEO, you thrive on those types of pressures.

The other thing I'd guess about your CEOship is that you're not a micro-manager. I could be way off on this one, but you seem to let us do what we do without interfering that often. Then again, some of us think you're involved in every small thing we do to the point of being a master puppeteer.

You as a puppeteer hasn't been my experience, but with your ability to get things done, you might be like some of the more wily people I've worked for who planted ideas in my head about what I ought to be doing and I didn't figure it out until six months after they'd sent me charging down the path unawares.

Some people think you are an absentee owner—completely hands off. I hope not. If that were the case, we'd send in the earnings and hope you didn't sell us off after one bad quarter.

The other thing I'd wonder about your role is how you treat competitors. Let's face it. You made it clear in the Bible that you were God and we weren't supposed to bring any other gods into the picture. Today we'd call that sort of leader a control freak or a megalomaniac. Control freaks and megalomaniacs don't tend to act the way you acted throughout the rest of the Bible. I mean, who would give up their son's life just to spare a bunch of ungrateful employees?

And understanding that I'm dealing with this issue from a human perspective, I don't think I've met a CEO yet who I'd be comfortable having in control of my life. Maybe this part of the analogy is where you separate yourself from any competitors.

Of course, I recognize the competitors you face don't often have faces. I'm not talking about evil which is real enough to me but which I don't understand well enough to begin asking about. I'm talking about that class of competitors known as "Distractions," all the possessions and status that are going to make our lives better if we can acquire more of them, be more accomplished in their use, or have them ascribed to us by others.

In telling us not to put any other gods before you, you mentioned all those specific Distractions that would interrupt our relationship with you and other people. I know you could put all those competitors out of business, but I sense from your management style that what you really want is for us to ignore them long enough for the free-market lifestyle you've granted to put them all out of business without your interference. I think you're trying to avoid an anti-trust situation.

I must say, after considering all these dizzying questions, I'm starting to think there's merit to taking a position on your team and letting you worry about the big-picture stuff. There is one issue I'd like to get resolved: Would you mind if I just worked for you a few days a week?

Dear God:
When you give someone a great vision, do you also make a campaign contribution?

OK. I did it. I put a bumper sticker on the back of my car. I've sworn I wouldn't openly support anyone for public office, especially the Big Office, but I got caught up in the heat of a primary election campaign, and I did. I'm not even sure if he's the right guy. It's time I came out of my political cave and stuck my neck out in favor of a candidate, so I did it, right or wrong.

Why do politics make me so cynical? Is it because I expect good things to happen even when the system those good things have to happen within generally promotes self-interest? Or is it because I want to believe so badly in something good that I find a rationale to support someone just as human as I am, even when I know that path is fraught with peril?

You know how much I believe in the power of vision—the ability to see out in the future and understand what needs to be done even when you don't know how to do it. The constant I've noticed in watching political campaigns is that candidates try to articulate their vision for the future as a way to win the hearts and minds of the voters. Sometimes it's education; sometimes it's political reform; sometimes it's growth; and sometimes it's some sort of undefined greatness, which these folks apparently possess in great measure.

God, most of them claim you as a source of guidance. I'm sure you'd like to be an integral part of each of the candidates' lives. How much of your earnestly sought input is real and how much is as fake as the promise of a huge tax cut without giving up any government benefits is another question, but that's for the electorate to find out after the election.

I'm wondering if you provide these visions to the elect of our fair land, and if so, do you also make a campaign contribution? Vision or not, to win an election takes money. In the case of politics, it's called putting your money where your mouthpiece is.

If you do decide to throw around some financial weight, there's something you should know. Donations can cause you problems with the government, particularly if your donation exceeded $1,000 and went straight to the candidate instead of some political action committee, but I think that, if you're big enough to give someone a great vision, you should be allowed to participate in the monetary side of the process as you see fit.

I'm not trying to be an alarmist, but, if your guy wins, you can bet any big contributions you make will wind up being the source of a Congressional investigation into illegal campaign practices. First, they'll note that you aren't an American citizen. They'd have conveniently forgotten this part if you'd given them the money instead of the other party. Then, they'll ask you what you wanted in return for the contribution. That may be your opportunity to shine.

In my idealistic way, you'd show up for the Congressional hearing without an attorney. As a matter of fact, you wouldn't make a grand entrance; You'd just suddenly be sitting there. When you were sworn in, of course you'd have to say, "So help me, me," which ought to warm things up in a hurry. I'm not sure how you'd handle a "state your occupation" question or a "place of residence" question though I prefer "Founding Father" and "everywhere" respectively. I think your appearance would make for fine drama on C-Span.

Obviously, I'm ignoring the fact that you don't make public

appearances in the conventional sense, but humor me a bit. I suspect you would, or more correctly, what I'd like to see you do, is begin with a statement reminding the assembled that you are the Creator of the Universe and that you aren't bound by the normal restrictions we place on people.

I'd also like to think that you'd hold up a coin and remind the assembled that their money declares our nation's trust in you and you're entitled to spend your share any way you please. I'd like to think at this point in the proceedings that sanity would prevail and the assembled would acknowledge you for who you are.

I'd like to think that obvious response would be the case, but it's more likely the hard-shelled cynicism that pervades the halls of government would dictate at least one person from the offended political party take a few cheap shots at you to see if you'd crumble. I can almost hear the question, "Do you understand that you've been called before the Senate of the United States of America?" Tell the good senator you *fully* understand.

Can nice people be in politics these days? It almost seems that, just by using the word "nice" in this context, it jumped off this page like a vegetarian at Rib Night. It seems to me political campaigns are like tough-man contests without actual blows being struck. Of course, the Bible reminds us the tongue can be used as readily as a sword. Perhaps politics *is* the ultimate tough-man rumble.

I have a problem with politics because I have the same sorts of expectations from people in public service as I have from you. The problem is that government isn't really any different from the people I work with every day. There are powerful people, some of whom abuse the privilege. There are ambitious people who are more than happy to run over any person in their path. There are bureaucrats who stamp, staple and keep the world moving. There are court followers who focus on staying attuned with the flavor-of-the-month mantra by spouting it at the appropriate times.

The difference is that I, we, most of us, expect government to be good and do good. I know it's silly, but many of us still think that "We the People" has some meaning.

With that expectation, and with more than a little experience of the other sort stored in our brains, we find it easy to be hypercritical when people act like people. We get excited when a candidate emerges from the pack with a message and image that stirs the faintly glowing embers of our cynical hearts—until he disappoints us. Our cynicism takes over, and we return to expecting little. When we expect little, that is generally what we receive.

Perhaps that's what's most wrong in our relationship with you as well. For us to acknowledge you as our Commander in Chief, we'd like you to fix all of our problems, thus freeing us of the responsibility to act as if we were created in your image. Of course, the Bible is full of your fixing the problems of the people of Israel, in a very hands-on manner and they turned from you anyway. In this great experiment of yours with us, you've learned we're not a very loyal lot, whether in politics or in following you.

I wish I could learn to expect more from you, but I'm afraid most of my priorities aren't connected to having you create the right life for me. It's a question of values, yours versus mine. Like some of the sticky questions of government, there's a price to be paid for every benefit. Often the short-term benefit is much easier to accept, rarely your way. But the short-term benefits make for great election fodder.

Let's return to this great vision idea. If anyone was really listening, what would you provide as a great vision for our country? Would this vision make your anointed electable? As a biblical sounding reference, the best I can think of is something like "if this people will humble themselves before me, I will prosper them." This statement sounds a little stilted today but it does cover the economic prosperity angle which has carried more than a few elections.

I'm not being fair. I know there are people who are deeply connected to you and who serve in government and who want to make the right choices for the right reasons. Making sure we're pursuing the right choices for the right reasons is a tough path to follow. People want simple answers. The right choice made for the right reason is seldom simple.

One aspect of political life I've noticed is that the really visionary people or those who give that appearance, seem to be on the far fringes of the political spectrum, and the following they attract is either very angry or very starry-eyed. They're looking to government for answers that exist elsewhere I'm afraid.

Where I'd like some help is in balancing the importance of the political process with my relationship with you. Government is probably as fine an example as there is of our looking to an imperfect institution to provide perfect answers. I know you work through imperfect people all the time, a good approach since there aren't any of the other type. I just hope you'll help me understand which imperfect person should carry your message every day as the leader of this country.

If I have the wrong bumper sticker on the car, could you loosen the adhesive a bit?

Dear God:
Do you ever call someone's house asking for their support?

I know you don't run for office, but you surely want our support. Since many of our political candidates have banks of people calling lists of names out of the voter registration files, it must be a good idea. Apparently, it doesn't matter that the person calling doesn't know me from Adam. Nor does it appear to matter that the caller is obviously reading a script that has no pauses for punctuation of any kind. It must be effective. The big boys do it. Why don't you?

You are in the business of reaching people and influencing their lives, are you not? You have often called people back to you, sometimes individually and sometimes *en masse*. So, if you really wanted to get people to think about you and consider their relationship with you, why not start up a phone bank, get a few volunteers and cut them loose with your script?

"Hi, this is Harvey Haufenberger calling on behalf of God. As you know, God created the world, including you and everything that's in it. His record and credentials are clear. God would like your support in bringing the world closer to him, so that through his vast experience and knowledge, the world could be made a much better place to live. But to realize this dream, he needs your help. You can help by telling your friends what a great God he is and asking them to join his campaign to bring the world back to him. You can also help by making a donation to the nearest homeless shelter in the name of God. Can I tell God that you support his efforts?"

It helps if you instruct the caller to use the gender of the person answering the call in referring to you. Those subtle touches go a long way. You might do some screening of the caller's ability to enunciate, pronounce your name correctly, stop for commas and periods, and otherwise act as though they have a little something on the ball.

So what do you think? Would it play in Peoria? I don't think so because I know how I feel when someone calls me with that sort of message from a political candidate. I feel annoyed and intruded upon even when the calls are for a candidate I support. It's as if I'm going to believe the Governor or the Senator actually asked this nice person to call me and seek my earnest support. I think the next time it happens that I'll ask the caller to send the Governor or the Senator by my house to spend ten minutes telling me why I should vote for them, and then I'll consider it.

The other reason I don't think it would play is that it's so absolutely impersonal. If you're not a personal God, frankly, I'm not sure what the point would be. If you were some distant, unreachable God, you wouldn't care about our drawing close to you anyway. We'd send you a letter sharing our concerns. You'd have your staff reply with a form letter thanking us for our input with your signature stamped neatly on the bottom.

A phone bank is not the way for you to go though many of us who grew up in some of your churches have been told all of our lives that if we'd go knock on a complete stranger's door and share the gospel you'd take care of the rest. I don't doubt that you could. It's been my experience that we generate as much resentment as curiosity, just as I feel when a third party calls me on the phone about supporting someone I've never met.

You want to change lives, right? As I see it, you change lives in two ways. You can either intervene directly in people's lives to the point they had no question you want their attention, or you can have the lives of all the people who claim you as their guiding source be lives that are worth copying.

There's a problem with either solution by itself. If all you did was intervene in people's lives in some unmistakable way, we'd all become conditioned to a sort of shock-treatment response to you, like Mr. Pavlov's dog. Now that invisible fencing has been invented, we'd wear a collar around our necks to tell us we were doing fine until we received a little or a big divine jolt. I know that's not what you want.

Perhaps, the bigger problem is that if you only operated through the lives of your followers, the undecideds out there would have a hard time figuring out if what you offer is much different from what they already have.

I suppose the answer is that some people need a jolt from you to understand their need for you, and there are enough of your people out there who represent you well enough to serve as a conduit for sparking interest in you.

In that sense, getting your message out is not so different from politics, is it? People have to be able to identify with the message and sense the rightness of it; then, they have to see that message proven in action. And, for some, the only way they'll get the message is when they have a problem so big and their despair is so great that they'll hook on to that message like a life raft.

In the human condition, desperate people tend to see the message in very simple terms of benefit without considering the consequences. In politics that's a very bad thing; in faith in you, it's a very mysterious thing. Sometimes the enormous act of turning our lives over to you brings consequences we'd never presuppose. The consequences aren't always rosy. It takes a great deal of trust to believe when the immediate path looks rocky. Truly trusting is the only step that removes fear from the unknowns that come from following. We can half-trust, but that doesn't open the door for the full range of possibilities.

So here we are. On the whole, we don't trust politicians, and, on the whole, we don't trust you very well either.

Another problem with politicians is that we tend to gather around them because of their perceived greatness even when they are as ripe for failure as the most common among us. While you don't carry around human weaknesses, all of your followers do. People who have received the greatest accolades as your human representative have fallen hard, and it gives you a bad name out there with those who are predisposed not to accept you in the first place. Not that it's your fault, but the chips fall where they may once people form opinions based on the actions of someone representing their leader. Pointing people to the real you might be tougher work than spinning a political disaster back into control.

You have an advantage. You have the knowledge, the qualifications, and the ability to change lives that none of us have. Help us understand that you have a personal interest in our best interests, whether we think your direction is best for us or not.

Here's what I'd like if it works for you. I'd like you to be my personal God, but I need some help. I'm so hardened by the reality of this world that I'm having trouble breaking through to you, or else you're having trouble breaking through to me. Are there some obstacles in my life you need to remove to improve our access to each other? I'm sure there are. I *do* need you in my life. Not the idea of you, but you.

I've already figured out that despite how bright you might have made me, I'm not smart enough to do a great or even a good job with my life. So feel free to knock on my door, or stop me in my tracks. I trust you to get it right. I know you're just having a hard time getting through to me right now.

One other thing. Please don't have some stranger call me on the phone seeking my support. It's you I want.

Dear God:
Are you a good loser?

I'm not.

I'll admit I'm not in a great mood. The reason I'm not in a great mood is I'm not a very good loser. You know how I've looked in the last hour, and you know what I've been thinking as well. For the most part, I haven't acted like a sore loser. But you know, down deep inside, I am a sore loser in this particular case, and my losing has brought on a flood of feelings inside that make me want to ask how you handle the agony of defeat. I don't like feeling the way I feel right now although I've felt it enough that I ought to be used to it. Can you give me some guidance?

You know the problem. After sticking my neck out with a simple bumper sticker, I see my guy losing with 38% of the vote counted. I can only remember feeling this way twice in my twenty-four years of voting. The first time I was eligible to vote I apparently picked the wrong candidate for President. The second time I backed someone (for state office) whom I knew against someone I had met and distrusted more than a little.

In both cases I felt the heat rising. I wondered how the majority of people could be so dumb as to elect someone so ill-suited for the job. Both individuals turned out to be one-termers and have since vanished from politics. I still haven't forgotten how it feels to be on the losing side.

Tonight has been a good reminder. I know it doesn't really matter, in the grand scheme of your universe, whether the guy I supported won or lost, but it bothered me to be on the losing side.

It hasn't helped my disposition that politics kicked in and people said untrue and exaggerated things about my guy. Untruths were spread by people whose campaign involvement was driven by a desire to set a "Christian agenda" for America. Neither has it helped my view that the other guy had the riches of King Solomon to spend on the campaign and should have won on that score alone.

Funny how the truth is such a rare and precious resource in a political campaign. It's not very funny that some of your people have sold their "religious" souls to get in bed with the politicians who wage these kinds of wars. Either Mark Twain or Abraham Lincoln or maybe neither said of someone, probably a politician, "He respects the truth so much he rarely uses it." Why do we have to hang your name on to such shenanigans?

Losing at something as irrelevant over the long run as a presidential primary race shouldn't have me this worked up. But it does.

So how does it feel when you lose? You do occasionally lose a battle here and there, don't you? The Bible is replete with stories of people taking a path other than yours even after you warned them not to do so. Weren't you angry? Didn't it make you want to swear off dealing with people forever?

There is the story of The Flood; then there's Sodom and Gomorrah; and there are a few others as well. As a matter of fact, the Bible says that you were very angry in a few cases. I mean really, really angry. A worldwide flood and destroying a couple of fair-sized cities is a pretty good sign of anger, is it not?

In both of these stories, you saved the few righteous. Who would be left if you picked the truly righteous in a political campaign? I know where you would find this person. You'd find that person in the single-digit category of a poll. It takes too much ambition to get elected, and ambition breeds compromise and a high level of aggression which doesn't strike me as falling on the side of righteousness.

But, you know what's in their hearts, and I don't. You know what's in their hearts, and you have a pretty good idea how they'll work out. We've had a pretty good run for some two centuries and two decades now even with some fairly incompetent and less-than-honest folks running the show. It's a tribute to our inclusive form of government. Eventually, momentum swings from the ridiculous back to the middle ground, and people go back to making money. But you already know that don't you?

I'd like you to help me get a better grasp on taking a longer-term view of life. You remember my third, fourth, and fifth grade teacher. She delivered one lesson I haven't forgotten. I can still hear her saying in that Low Country brogue, "My father always told me there were three sides to an argument: my side, your side, and the right side."

Maybe I should have learned from all the wisdom that razor-sharp brain of hers carried around. Maybe I should learn that losing your temper over inconsequential things doesn't lead to the most productive of lives. Just maybe, I should even consider that I can't hold all the answers because I don't see inside people's hearts the way you do, so that it's better to suspend judgment and await the outcome more often than not.

If I can trust you to help me learn those attributes in some sustainable way, will you let my guy win the next time around?

Dear God:
Do you catch much
clear-channel radio?

God, the one thing that seems to cover as wide an area as you and McDonald's are clear channel radio stations. As a child, I learned to love clear channel radio stations at night because they took me to romantic places I'd never been, including some that don't seem nearly as romantic anymore: Ft. Wayne, Chicago, and New Orleans. They were a world away in my twelve-year old view of life.

Those were the last glory days of AM radio. Then, the only place to catch Top 40 or a dash of rock and roll at night was on the AM side of the dial. It came from a thousand miles away. I remember listening in my bedroom to WLS in Chicago while my seven-years-older-sister held a New Year's Party at our house. The specific memory that sticks is of a DJ named John Landecker and "The Immigrant Song" by Led Zeppelin. My prized Sharp AM/FM Cassette, with its ability to tape songs from the radio, was a fine coup for a twelve-year old. I'd listen to the music and then the weather, which around New Year's in Chicago, was a 10-degree trip to a frozen paradise.

What did you think of me back then? Did you know all the ups and downs of my life that were coming? Did you see my teen years and realize I'd be a combination of good and not so good, or was that all up in the air? I wonder these things now that I'm over forty. Back then, having a leg up on the rest of my world by listening to a station out of Chicago was good enough.

You remember earlier this week I made a nighttime drive to Charleston. South of Columbia, the traffic thinned, and the FM side of the dial became too repetitive after two hours on the road. I hit the AM button and the search mode. The only station that came in was running a service from a black church. I never caught the name of the church or the location of the station, but I caught the spirit of worship that made me envy the freedom that was jumping out of the speakers. After two hours of rock, country, easy listening, and commercials, it was like settling back into another world, where the only object was to raise the roof on your behalf. Then, the signal faded.

I hit search again, and another call sign from the past had enough juice to halt the LCD display at 15.10 AM. WLAC, Nashville. 15LAC. A flood of memories rushed in from another time when I was an eighteen year-old college freshman. On the way back to school in East Tennessee, WLAC's clear channel signal flooded into the mountain passes. Now, WLAC appears to be a talk station, the fate of AM nationwide. This particular night, the fine Tennessee fans were questioning Jerry Green's manhood, mental capacity, and dressing habits after a loss to Vanderbilt.

But even with that noise, I found myself in another time and a much younger body. Somewhere around Orangeburg, it became 1976 again. It was late fall in the mountain passes of Western North Carolina and East Tennessee. A Sunday night with the utter darkness that mountain roads hold.

I remembered the anguish of leaving home to go back to a place I hadn't quite taken to for some reason or the other. I remembered a girlfriend at home and a week ahead of getting by on a few dollars. I also remembered how good four hot dogs for a dollar tasted at the local joint there in my college town, and I thought about giving plasma in Knoxville for seven dollars to have a little spending money. I thought about a blonde-haired girl I asked out later that year. We ran out of gas on the way back from Knoxville in a borrowed car with a stuck gas gauge in a pouring February rain. I never asked her out again.

I thought about many things, and I was sad for a bit. Sad for a place where I was never very happy but in recollection had my share of friends and more than my fair share of good times. But I also remembered the isolation of trying to fit in somewhere new. I wondered what had happened along the way in my life to lead me to where I was at that current moment in time, on that dark interstate with a four- or five-hundred-mile-away radio station as my only company.

As I reflected, I didn't think about where you were in those days. Back then, I didn't think about you very much. I knew you were there. I just didn't think about you as more than an accepted, but abstract, part of my life.

What I felt as I drove was a longing for a time long gone, and I can't imagine why unless that time was less complicated or perhaps I was just less complicated. I had less of everything in those days: self confidence, sound reasoning, money, and acknowledgment of me as being just fine from my friends, but, it was also a time when the future seemed forever, and the options for what my life would be were all good.

I find myself going back to those days more and more lately as my child grows older and as I start to realize that fifty isn't too awfully far away anymore. I realize that with fifty years of life a few exits down the road, the youth I've held on to for so long is starting to slip away. Yes, you know I've considered my mortality more and more of late, and you've seen me changing my diet and taking vitamins and doing all sorts of things to try to guarantee I'll be around here long enough not to make turning fifty such a big deal.

I guess staring at my mortality is at the heart of what I really want to know. What is it you want me to do with the rest of my life, now that there may be less of it left than what came before? I've been having this question wander around in my mind for a couple of years now. I think it's because I climbed as close to the top as I was going to get and thought, "the view's not that much better. Surely, there's more to it than this."

I want a legacy. I hope, in particular, that it includes being a good parent who produced a child who accomplishes twenty times more than I did because that's the only big legacy I'll leave unless you give me the wisdom to do more than I've done so far. But I'd like it to go further.

Somewhere deep inside, I have this idea that you want me to do all sorts of marvelous things with my life if we can both get pointed in the same direction which I guess is the heart of the problem. My direction and yours haven't been in synch for a while, and I'll be darned if I can figure out what I'm supposed to do to get back on the right track.

We've talked about this issue more than a little, and I feel like I'm beating my head against a wall more often than not. I'm in a rush to be whatever it is I'm supposed to be well before I reach fifty. My haste comes from wasting so much time up until now. I've got to move, get it going, head down the path.

You know where I'd like to be right now. I'd like to be comfortable in a financial sense. I'd like to work because I choose to and not because I have to. I wouldn't mind having a place at the beach, and I'd like to be thirty pounds lighter and still look like I'm twenty-five from a distance. I'd like to be, and have, all those things, but I don't think you're very interested in any of them.

I know, based on the times I felt most tuned in to you, that you can show me another world that doesn't include any of those things but is far more interesting. Would you show me that world? Would you help me see how I can turn my apprehension about the approaching years into a race to get all the good stuff done you want me to do? Just don't tell me I'm doing those things right now. If I am, fifty won't get here soon enough.

Perhaps the next time I'm on the road at night and pick up a clear channel signal from the past, you'll help me understand how everything that has occurred in my life to date is a preparation for doing all the things I could be doing until my time here is through. Perhaps you'll do that for me. I need the encouragement, and I need your focus.

By the way, my son has found at twelve the same fascination with picking up a long-distance signal at night from a faraway, romantic place. I hope you'll help me find your signal isn't as far away as I've come to believe. It's not much good if I can only receive it at night in the middle of nowhere.

Dear God:
Have you ever listened to the words to "Comfortably Numb?"

I can't see you as a Pink Floyd fan, but, since you are all knowing and all-a-lot-of-other-things, I figure you've picked up on the lyrics at some time or the other. If you *are* a Pink Floyd fan, I'll have some of my questions answered about the mysteries of the universe. I'll also have just as many new questions.

I only ask this question because I developed a very serious taste for this song almost twenty years after it was released, and I'd like to try to tell you why. I'm not sure this will be a simple task, but neither is figuring out Pink Floyd's music at times. What I'm really trying to say is that the song intrigues me. You remember the first time I heard this song, don't you? I was driving home from Charlotte four years ago, and it came on the radio. I was transfixed, not by the overall story told by the lyrics, because I didn't remember but one line, "I've become... comfortably numb."

"Comfortably numb." What a telling phrase. I had never been much of a Pink Floyd fan, nor had I ever been curious to know which one was pink. But it's surprising, given my love of music, that in the sixteen years the song had been around, I'd failed to hear it. I heard it that night, and three or four times a year since then. Each time I heard it, I never really caught any of the lyrics but that one line, that, the orchestration, and the piercing guitar licks.

Isn't it interesting that a song created when I was senior in college, fully available to me all this time, never touched my life until I was thirty-eight-years old and fully engaged in trying to earn a living 100 miles of interstate from home? Don't you think it's a bit bizarre that of all the music I've listened to over those years, "Comfortably Numb" never once crossed paths with me until that very point in time? Maybe you don't think it's odd. Maybe not.

At that point in time I *was* comfortably numb, not necessarily in the context of the song, but in the context of a life I'd accepted and gone about numbly to keep from feeling all the pain running around inside me. I had the necessary barriers fully raised, and I floated through my dual existence between towns. I heard it in the song, I realized what it meant for me, and I pushed it away and just kept plodding forward in a meandering straight line of nothingness. That single song title brought it home for me. Yet, it took me several years to do anything about it.

You'll also remember during that time my numbness was supplanted with anger. Part of my anger was directed at you. I know now that my anger at you was a way to hold on to my numbness, a way to keep from feeling and moving forward. But numbness is comfortable when you don't want to confront your life. It's very comfortable until something pierces the numbness.

As you know, I finally broke down and bought *The Wall* a few months back as a Christmas present to myself. Of course, the first track I listened to was track six on the second CD of the set. I've listened to it at least fifty times since then, and the rest of the CD as well. I now understand the lyrics and the context of the song in *The Wall* and it's more intriguing than ever.

The song is actually about an all-too-familiar topic in the music world—a musician so saturated with the double-edged sword of success that his body only responds to a needle to make it on stage the next night. You know that in my life, and I assume in other lives, there are plenty of needles to go around to make us get up and pretend every morning. Pretending is good stuff as long as nothing punctures the bubble.

So, what do you think about "Comfortably Numb?" Is it a song about a burned-out musician, or is it a bigger look at the many lives you see every day? Are there a lot of people out there like me who pull out a metaphorical needle to get through the day more often than they'd like to admit? I'd like to know. I'd like to know because this particular subject cuts deep into our spirits, and most of us aren't very good about discussing this subject with others, unless we're paying someone $75 an hour. I'm afraid more of us than not are just existing, that we lack purpose and passion. Isn't that comfortably numb?

I suspect from being on the fringes of other lives that many people would relate to the song that way, particularly if they heard it under the right circumstances. In religious circles, we're generally told how happy we ought to be, but I know enough about many people's lives to know the show they might put on each Sunday is yet another needle stop. They're confused and stressed and tired and a little afraid. Most of them look at their lives and think it just hasn't turned out the way they planned.

I put on my "Sunday-go-to-meeting" face this morning and went to Sunday School. You know our teacher better than me, an honorable man who works hard at presenting the lesson well. He caught me in a contrary mood, and I ended up questioning some basic facts about the way life ought to be versus the way life is.

We talked about the Book of Revelations. I'm not exactly sure what you meant with that one, but it's a little like Pink Floyd—much easier to deal with the general effect than trying to interpret all the details. In this case, the details are hard to understand, hard to swallow, and pretty difficult to interpret to be honest. Many people over time have made the effort to interpret, and, on this particular Sunday, the interpretation included the idea that John, the receiver of the revelation, was trying to encourage the churches of the day, many of whom were under extreme persecution, to hold the course, renew their faith, and look for your promised return.

In all that explanation, a verse jumped out that seemed out of synch with my understanding of Your Church. These persecuted churches cried out for you to bring justice against their persecutors, to even the score. I was troubled that in the early church, as in society today, the cry was, "Even the score." That verse didn't sit well with me. Two thousand years later, Christians are still trying to even the score with those who oppose us. The only difference today is that we want the score evened legislatively.

Anyone who grew up in the Christian tradition learns the model of the early church: sharing their possessions with each other, believing in and receiving miracles, spreading the word. At the same time, what it was (and you know this better than I), was a group of people, just like me, looking for hope. Sometimes they felt hopeless. I felt the need to bring up that point during our class. I hope you didn't mind, but it just jumped out at me that the church model of the New Testament was as often filled with pain and doubt as we are today.

I was reminded of something else that came out of Revelation. Jesus told the church at Laodicea, if I'm not mistaken, that they "were neither hot nor cold", and for that reason he would "spit them out of (his) mouth." Is neither "hot nor cold" something like being "comfortably numb?" Are we living lukewarm lives because we can't figure out anything else to do?

This question is a serious one. I remember a piece of dialogue I once heard where a searching question about purpose was firmly answered, "ours is to endeavor to persevere." It must have been something British. I'm afraid that too often that statement has more than a ring of truth to it. Endeavor to find strength to put up with all of it, but never, never rise above it all. I'll persevere in my faith and my daily life because the alternative isn't that great, but I wonder if there's some missing ingredient that can take me from persevering to living. Would you help me out there?

I have one more question for you. Do you work through all sorts of things to help us see what we need to see? More specifically, do you work through people, events, and such that we normally wouldn't associate with you? Did you speak to me through that song? Was the song there waiting for the right time for me to hear it before I finally did? Or is it just coincidence that I heard it at a point in life when my receptors were very attuned to a revelation of a different kind?

I'm not going to buy any more Pink Floyd music in hopes of catching an insight. *The Wall* is enough for me. But, I might try tuning in to some of your other frequencies if they're open in all the most unexpected places.

I do love the song; I just don't want to live my life in parallel.

> "When I was a child I caught a fleeting glimpse,
> out of the corner of my eye.
> I turned to look but it was gone.
> I can not put my finger on it now,
> the child is grown, the dream is gone.
> I've become....comfortably numb."
> —Comfortably Numb, Pink Floyd, The Wall, 1979

Dear God:
Is it better to be the king or the kingmaker?

In human terms, who really runs the world? Is it the kings or the kingmakers? I've learned there are the people out front, and then there are the people actually in charge, pulling the strings, making the calls. But you already know that.

I'm not talking about this phenomenon that kicks up in literature every now and then; some variation on a tightly held conspiracy by a few, very private, very powerful men controlling all the major decisions of the world, starting a war as needed to balance things out; that sort of thing. For all I know, that may be true, but that type of scenario is way past my comprehension. I'm talking about those everyday functions of government or business, or, for that matter, the Little League, where someone appears to be in charge but more often than not has some very solid but less visible influences guiding their direction.

You *know*. I just *suspect*. What's the deal? Who's actually in charge?

Maybe it doesn't matter in the grand scheme of things. People still go to work, get married, have children, retire, and die. And I suppose no matter who's in charge from a human perspective, those things will keep happening. Perhaps there are very subtle, but important, influences being exerted all the time from a human perspective, and we've just learned to live within their bounds.

In fact, there are more than a few who think the church is one of the greatest conspiracies of recorded history and a way to keep people safely in the bounds of a functioning society. There might be some truth to that idea, particularly when the church functions as an arbiter of human behavior rather than as a facilitator of your love and grace. You know at my core I'm not a conspiracy type. I don't see threats behind every corner though I will admit I've learned there's enough evil floating around to keep us suspended between faith and fear.

What I generally see happening around me are the daily acts of people just trying to get along in their lives. Every now and then, I decide to take on something of great importance to me and find there's a whole spectrum of influence and power I don't understand at all, and I begin to wonder if it's possible to live in your light and get things done without being contaminated by the process.

What I'm really after is how human power is actually gained. I'm afraid I know, but I'm hoping you'll help me understand from your perspective. After all, you see the Big Picture. I see the parts and pieces.

What I have experienced is that the world turns based on the subtleties of influencing other people to do what one person or group of people want done. At its worst, we've seen the power of Nazi Germany or even regimes today that repress and kill with the implicit consent of the people. Unfortunately, we rally behind emotional issues, made more emotional when a perceived threat to our autonomy or our prosperity is brought to our attention. In responding to the threat, we sometimes give power to people who are pulling our emotional strings.

I'd like to go beyond being manipulated. I'd also like to understand how I can work within human systems to get things done that are in keeping with what you'd want done. What I don't want is to be contaminated with the power that often comes out of succeeding.

We've talked about the danger of power before. You know

I've talked with other people about this topic as well. I like having control of my life. I like influencing the lives of other people, hopefully in a positive way. I've seen the dark side of power, and I don't ever want to be in its grip, either as a transmitter or receiver of it.

I believe power is the greatest motivator in the world. Asked to name the greatest motivator of people, some folks would say sex, some money, and some fame or position. I think power, or the perception of power, is what makes us do what we do more often than anything else. In other words, we like playing you. I'm not a psychiatrist so maybe I ought to leave the analysis alone.

What I am is somebody who would like to make a difference. What I see is that, in making a difference, there's a choice to be made. That choice involves either living within some tightly defined parameters of lines that can't be crossed or choosing to do whatever is necessary to accomplish our goal. There's a price to be paid either way.

If I live within tightly defined parameters, my ability to influence is weakened. If I have an "at all costs" attitude, I'll end up paying somebody at some point to whom I'd rather not be indebted at all.

I asked you if it was better to be the king or the kingmaker. Is it better to be the king and have favors to bestow and favors expected? Or, is it better to be the kingmaker and have the right to call in debts as needed? You know that I've met some kings, except that none of them were called kings. They were called Senator or Representative or Mayor or Judge or something else of the sort. And I've met some of the people who were responsible for putting those particular monarchs in their positions. They're usually called Mister. I don't want to be either if that's the price. I do want to make a difference.

Is it possible to be the king without being a political debtor? I recently read a quote that said, "If you swim with the sharks, there's going to be blood in the water." Is doing something of merit conditional upon getting in the water? Can I make a difference without getting my feet wet?

Is it possible to be neither king nor kingmaker and still make a difference? Is it possible to walk a tightrope between neither owning or owing?

I'm afraid the answer strikes at the core of what moves us forward: power. I'm afraid that answer is contained in your word, and I'm afraid the answer was provided by your very best example. I'm afraid the answer is Jesus. Yes, I'm afraid, because he was one of a kind, wouldn't you say? Living within the parameters of your answers means that I, or anyone else for that matter, has some pretty big shoes to attempt to fill.

Jesus is your example of literally having all the power in the world and only using it to do your work. Jesus is your example of being powerful, wise, and compassionate all at the same time. That's a very tough answer, God, a very tough answer indeed.

You see, for us Jesus is a very tough answer because living in his footsteps requires giving up a lifestyle that seems important for a lifestyle that doesn't seem important, but is. It requires looking into the lives of unloveable people, both powerful and powerless, and seeing a trace of your likeness imprinted somewhere on their being. It requires that we relinquish power to have it. Those are pretty tough requirements.

No, I don't want to be the king or the kingmaker. I don't want either, but, I do want to have the strength, the wisdom, the compassion, and the courage to make a difference. Perhaps you'll give me a measure of each of those that I can handle. And along the way, perhaps you'll help me recognize the difference between being powerful and power-giving, the difference between being influential and effective, the difference between being admired and respected, the difference between doing your work and doing my own.

Dear God:
Will we ever see the
Hardy Boys again?

In nearly a year of getting reacquainted with the Hardy Boys, I've seen them solve *The Tower Treasure* mystery, *The Shore Road* mystery, *The House on the Cliff* mystery and several other mysteries without aging a bit. Frank and Joe and their typecast friends are once again foiling the criminal interests of Bayport.

As you know, I'm reliving my childhood once again through my son. We're now on Book 11 of the Hardy Boys. I don't remember the name of the book we've just started. We only made it to page six tonight before he fell asleep. But already, Chet has caught grief about his appetite and resulting girth, Biff remains his well-cut athletic self, and Frank and Joe continue to move with the assurance of thirty-year veterans of the police force.

Is this childhood fantasy a sign of a different time?

Ah, the Hardy Boys, and their well-groomed, good-looking cast: their father, Fenton Hardy, the tall, handsome famous former detective on the New York City police force; their mother Laura, "a slender, attractive woman;" Aunt Gertrude, Mr. Hardy's severe, spinster sister; and, of course, Joe and Frank's steady dates: Chet's attractive and apparently unbulky sister Iola; and Callie Shaw, beautiful and admiring.

Doesn't fiction sound so much better than reality? Do you know anyone who actually resembles the Hardy family and friends in looks, attitude, and brains? If you do, I don't want to know them, because I'd be very uncomfortable around that much perfection. My son picked up on this golden scene, recognizing the stereotypes without my prompting, something I never grasped at his age.

Is it good or bad that he already has enough cynicism or realism or whatever to see past the basic story line? Or was I prepped for an idyllic life during my early days and didn't realize that life doesn't much work out that way at all? I don't know the exact period when these books were published, but they were obviously written at a time when people dreamed of perfection in their families, a time when cynicism and doubt didn't plague the majority of the population, and when more Americans went to church than not, whether it was through social convention or an act of faith. Nope, I don't see much of the Hardy Boys these days.

My son watched me drop my question to you on to this page last night and felt the need to inform me that some new Hardy Boys mysteries had been published in the 90's. I'm not sure I want to read those tales. I'm afraid of the mysteries that might be handed to Frank and Joe.

The first thing I'm sure of is that Frank and Joe wouldn't live through the first mystery. They're captured by the bad guys in almost every book, yet manage to escape from being tied-up, locked inside a cave filled with explosives, left to drift out to sea on an abandoned boat, or face some other peril from which escape seems impossible, yet they always make it out to detect again. Today, they'd have been shot on the spot and become a short-lived detective team, leaving their father on a lifelong quest seeking vengeance against a drug cartel or a corrupt politician.

Have we reached an age where we're telling the truth about the way things actually are and have been for most of human history, or, have we all just gotten a little too rotten for our own good? Do the Hardy Boy represent a culture that's gone for good, or were we just better at pretending thirty years ago?

One thing I'm sure of—over the last five years or so, there has been an increasing trend of people displaying their very worst tendencies without feeling the need to apologize. I'm not sure where this trend started or what or who is responsible, but it has become fashionable to be less than normal if normal can be characterized anymore. At the same time, the statistics show that the nuclear family of the Hardy Boys variety is now a minority in the population. We don't see good old-fashioned fist fights in school anymore. We see people with weapons, and those weapons are used randomly more than any of us like to consider.

But, you know what? (Yes, of course, you do.) I like some elements of this open society and apparently so do many other people. I don't like sweeping issues of substance under the rug with the idea that if the better people among us don't think about them, they'll cease to exist. I don't like pretending that families are perfectly content, when during the time the Hardy's roamed the streets of Bayport, there were miserable people who didn't want to let anyone know just how miserable they were. The Hardy's never ran out of criminals to fight did they?

What I don't like very much about our tell-all society is that it has become a breeding ground for people to excuse almost any type of behavior. As a society, we've gone from not talking about our problems to talking about our problems, and then making excuses for the problems we're talking about.

Over a century ago, progress in science and technology began to lead people to think that mankind was on the verge of solving its most perplexing issues. We aren't there. Things might be getting worse. Then, again, things might not be getting worse, but we're certainly hearing more about them because people aren't keeping their deepest problems to themselves anymore. I am pretty sure that things aren't getting better. We're still people, acting like people, and there are more of us to act like people than at any time in history. On top of this multiplying effect, there are more ways for us to learn that people are acting like people, whether we want to know or not know in many cases.

Did you like the Hardy Boys' world better than this one? Was

Leave It To Beaver your idea of a good time? Or, do you find the mix and match world we live in today equally promising? Some prophets of doom think you're going to end it all pretty soon. Given biblical prophecy about "the end times," it looks as if we've done a spectacular job of late in driving you toward action.

I wonder. I wonder if you do your best work when things look the worst. The New Testament church thrived in an openly pagan society. Its steady decline from a true extension of you came after it was legalized and institutionalized into the various governments that owned it.

Maybe you're ready to do something big again. Maybe this change in society's makeup is actually a path to people truly finding you and not being institutionalized into a prescribed human system of worship and faith. Maybe you're going to take all of the pain and bring light out of it. Maybe you're stacking up for your grand finale. Maybe.

The one thing I feel certain of, given history, is that you want people to do your work, and that begs another question. What kind of people do you want? Do you want the ones who have clung to the institutions of the Hardy Boys' days, or do you want people who like being open but not the results of it? Or do you want all of us? Do you want me and the other guy with all our imperfections, with our sanctimonious black hearts and our openly black hearts to find your voice in the cacophony of opinions that bounce off every mountain today?

I'm betting you want all of us. It seems so very you to take the bleakest situations and bring good out of them. It takes you to push aside all the barricades we've erected against you and show us the part of our being that represents your image.

Here's your challenge. Your World is a very polarized place. We like labels because they help us identify friend and foe: liberal or conservative for one. Today, we all have to be one or the other. I wish I could find which one was endorsed in the Bible.

How are you going to bring us all together? I don't think you intend for us to be apart. Is it through the lives of children? Are they the last unpolluted creatures on earth? Is it our job to put aside the things that divide us to raise a generation that believes responsibility and compassion can work side by side?

The Bible shows you let generations pass in complete defiance of you. It also shows you brought good into play before the final curtain dropped. I hope you'll help us to see that all of the baggage we carry as adults doesn't have to be transferred to younger shoulders. Show us that, despite our differences, the lives of those who follow us depend on each of us working in your image.

And if you can help us see those things, I might not find the Hardy Boys such a tough sell anymore.

Dear God:
What were that man and his dog doing on the side of the road yesterday?

You know who I'm talking about: the middle-aged, nondescript guy and his leashed lap dog, car parked on the side of the road, with man and dog strolling around in the grass. I assume he was letting the dog out to use the bathroom. But that was a very strange location for a bathroom break so I think there was more there than meets the eye.

Let's set the scene so that I'm sure we're talking about the same person. No doubt quite a few thousand people were giving their dog some relief on the side of the road at the moment I passed this particular duo. While the number of owners and dogs stationed on the side of the road at any one time makes for an interesting snapshot of modern society, it was this particular geographic spot that piqued my interest.

I'm talking about the guy just up the road from my house, 100 yards from the four-lane, who apparently had to stop right there to let Fido and nature take their consensual course. I know that dogs are like children: Put them in a car and when they have to go, they have to go. But why there? This was a spot where nobody on a long trip would wind up. This was a spot that's a pass-through area for people coming from houses one, two, and three miles away. But this guy was there, letting his dog sniff around outside a building that houses a chemical distributor. It just seemed so out of place with the reality I've come to expect of that piece of formerly clean dirt.

Now, you know that in my laziness, I've pulled over on that same spot to let the ice melt from the windshield of the car. It's almost exactly one mile from our house, and I've stopped there several times after driving blindly for a mile and finally admitting the defroster isn't going to kick in that quickly on a cold morning. Would I stop to let my dog out there, leash in hand? I don't think so.

I think there's much more to this story than meets the eye. I'd like to try out a few theories. Let me know if I'm getting warm.

I think the guy took the dog over to his former girlfriend's house in an attempt to earn his way back into her good graces. She met him at the door, told him to get lost; he left with a squirming whiner in his car.

Not that one, huh?

How about this scenario? His girlfriend or wife kicked him out, telling him to "take that sorry mutt" with him. Two miles from her house, the dog started scratching his Corinthian leather seats, and he knew it was time for a pit stop.

Is that it? Pets have been door openers and closers for more relationships than the ultimate owner of the pet would care to admit. He looked pretty silly out there with Fido doing his business that close to a residential area. He'd gotten the boot, had he not?

No? What about this one?

The guy was going to be reunited with his parents after years of estrangement. He'd led a wayward life for fifteen or twenty years and was finally returning home for the prodigal reunion, but, they'd moved. He's left with his only friend in the world in the midst of unfamiliar turf, so to speak; hence, his stop at the one wide shoulder in this narrow road.

Or, maybe his parents misunderstood his call to them and thought he was coming the week after they took the Retirement Club tour bus to Branson. He's down to his last $40, enough gas money to get back to Florida, where most wayward people wind up in this part of the world. Sadly, the only evidence of his being there is left by his dog two miles down the road. The hastily scrawled note he left between the door and the door jamb blew away in the afternoon breeze and was later picked up by the litter volunteers who periodically make a sweep of the area.

Not that either? What about this?

He's all by himself in this world. Riding down that stretch of road, he spots the fur ball looking lost. He stops, picks the dog up, and realizes a mile later that the dog doesn't much like riding in cars. But that doesn't explain the leash.

How about this idea?

He and his dog ride the roads every Saturday. After a shared breakfast of eggs and toast and bacon, they hit the road in search of, well, other roads. Countless hours are whiled away as man and beast, with nose to the wind, tour the highways and byways of Greenville County with an occasional exotic foray into the wilds of Spartanburg. They stop for lunch at McDonalds, in the playground area, of course. By midafternoon, they're exhausted by the travails of the day and return to their small cottage for a nap and an evening of watching *Lassie* and *Rin-Tin-Tin* together.

You won't even comment on that one, will you?

What *were* they doing there? No person with good sense would need to stop at that place to let his dog use the bathroom.

Oh, that's it! He was actually taking his wife's dog to the vet and the little rascal started scratching around and he hadn't taken the dog out in the yard before he left even though he'd promised his wife he would? Oh, I see.

That's so very ordinary. That's what was going on?

I'm really disappointed. I was making a trip to the pet supply store for some more dog food. I really thought I'd glimpsed some very bizarre behavior, or maybe even a classic example of some pitiful life being lived out on the side of the road.

Do you know how much better I felt seeing this guy having to stop at that spot to take his dog to the bathroom? At that moment in time, I was one-up on at least one other person in this part of the world. I was cruising along in an '88 LeSabre, free as the breeze, and here's some bozo having his life run by seven pounds worth of dog.

I have to admit that life is much more interesting when there's someone else out there having a more miserable time of it than I am. Here I was on the way to pay $35 for forty pounds of dog food which my own hound will eat only when he's certain there aren't any more table scraps coming his way, and this guy, this poor guy, is having to stop on the fringe of a residential area, off the main path of commerce, to let his dog take care of business.

Funny how we form such instant opinions about someone, isn't it? I hope the people who have seen me stopped there in the morning to let the car defrost were in such a hurry to get to work that they didn't wonder how stupid one human being could be to attempt driving a car with only four square inches of clear glass to see through.

Dear God:
What part of "no tomatoes" sounds like a foreign language anywhere I get carry out?

I'm a victim in this case. I don't like tomatoes. I'll eat them cooked in spaghetti sauce if the chunks aren't too big. I'll eat them in salsa. I'll eat them in many cooked but heavily pureed forms, but I don't eat them in their natural state. Remember how the first settlers to the New World thought they were poisonous? You had to let them find out otherwise. Now, I'm hung with the stigma of being a tomato opponent.

It's been this way since I've been old enough to order for myself. "I'd like the jumbo cheeseburger, no tomatoes." Five minutes later, I have a cheeseburger with tomatoes. Somehow the words, "no tomatoes," spoken from my mouth, sail into the ether, never to be seen again. I expect to get tomatoes even though I specifically, directly, and unequivocally ask that they be left off the dish in question.

With culinary changes, I've also had to begin asking that chopped eggs be left off salads in establishments where that sort of thing is apparently considered *haute cuisine*. But I don't eat at those places often so that the egg thing isn't a big deal. Plus, I get perverse pleasure in asking that the salad be taken back, just because it came from a place that was haughty enough to think that diced, chopped, whatever-they-are eggs should be placed on a salad in the first place.

But the ubiquitous tomato, that's another story. I've picked them from nachos grande. I've tossed them from grilled chicken salads. I've extracted them from 99-cent cheeseburgers and $6.95 cheeseburgers. I told you I didn't buy conspiracy theories, but I'm pretty sure there's a massive conspiracy on the part of the tomato growers of the world to shatter my nerves.

Admittedly, it hasn't been as bad lately. The good news is that, if you go to the same two or three restaurants once a week for five years, they'll figure out that you don't like tomatoes and manage to leave them from your order.

But last week, oh, last week. I went to two of these establishments and ordered. At the first place, "I'd like the jumbo cheeseburger, no tomato, with onion rings instead of fries, a chili sandwich on a hamburger bun, plain, and a tea, to go." Same order I've given the last twenty-seven times I have gone in the place. These folks don't write down the order. They just stare directly into your eyes while you're giving it and then spit out a stream of words that are normally spoken around the Mediterranean.

As I watched my cheeseburger being assembled, I cast a suspicious eye to the metal bowls that hold lettuce, onion, and The Unspeakable. I saw it coming. After slathering on the mayonnaise, he reached for The Bowl. Out plopped a slimy slice of tomato, and on to the bun it went.

"Excuse me," I said. We locked eyes. "Is that my cheeseburger you're fixing?" A monosyllabic affirmation followed. "I asked for no tomatoes." No response, but the tomato is deftly lifted from the bun and tossed back into the tomato holder.

Did you know any time that happens, three or four tomato seeds cling for life to my cheeseburger? You must have made those little rascals very hearty because they'll stick to anything. Nuclear holocaust would kill every living organism except tomatoes and mosquitoes.

Three days later, I ventured into my favorite Mexican restaurant. I made a mistake. I ordered something beside the number one combination, which contains no tomatoes. I ventured far out on the ledge and ordered a fajita-like concoction that places nacho chips all along the bottom of the dish, sort of like nachos grande with chicken strips added.

With their normal grace, my order was accepted and rushed to the kitchen. I was back out the door in less than ten minutes. Upon arriving home, I pulled the cardboard lid from the aluminum plate that sequesters their carry-out offerings and found a massive chunk of tomatoes ensconced directly in the middle of this South-of-the-Oklahoma-border delicacy.

I lost it. I didn't say anything vile, but I did place the cardboard on top, fold the edges of the aluminum plate over to hold it in place and head out the door to the restaurant. I suggested to my wife that she continue eating her meal. Fortunately for her, tomatoes are one of the food groups she likes.

Upon arriving at the restaurant, I waited my turn at the cashier and then presented my tomato-stained dinner to him. He apologized and began making out a gift certificate. "Hold on. I want a refund." My firmness caused a pause. Then he opened the cash register and fished out $6.50, give or take twenty cents.

God, you saw all of this happen, and you know that deep down inside I was more than a bit piqued by this failure on the part of one of my favorite meal providers. I don't think I acted badly. You know I wouldn't in front of people whom I genuinely like so much anyway.

Why do I get so upset over something as silly as tomatoes? Am I programmed that way? Is there something in my genetic code that makes me abhor that particular vegetable in its rawest state? I don't think so because you know my parents would rather eat tomatoes than filet mignon. My sister eats them and acts happy about it.

I remember I used to feel the same way about potato salad. I think it was the texture which, when fixed a certain way, isn't much different from the way a tomato feels in your mouth. Of course, some people put egg whites in potato salad. Perhaps that explains that problem.

Or, is it that I've had them thrust upon me against my explicitly stated wishes for so long that I activate the postal gene passed down from my retired letter-carrier father as soon as someone defies my wishes?

I don't know. Frankly, I'm embarrassed. As well I should be, I suppose. There are some things I don't tolerate very well, tomatoes in my food for one. At some point a person has to take a stand. Since getting decent service in restaurants is now like trying to pick seven correct numbers in the lottery, maybe I'm justified in drawing a line in the counter grease.

Do you look at me when I act this way and shake your head? After all, I've botched a few of your explicit directions, all of which are were much more important than a slice of tomato mistakenly slapped on a cheeseburger.

Yes, I suspect you must shake your head and perhaps chuckle just a bit. After all, you'd be blowing your stack all the time if it came down to the tomatoes we slip into your order.

Should I give in and learn to eat tomatoes? Or, should I just order the number one combination from this point forward?

I imagine life would be pretty predictable if I stuck with the number one combination. If I'm looking for something outside the predictable, it would probably be helpful if I learned to treat the tomatoes that jump in my path with a little less concern and ordered fewer number one combinations and a few more specials of the day.

Isn't that where you come in? Do you take all the tomatoes in our lives and help us learn to deal not only with them but to relish their appearance? Are you in charge of breaking down the barriers of tomato intolerance? Is there great treasure to be found in a tomato?

I don't want to like tomatoes, and I suppose it doesn't much matter whether I eat them or not or even whether someone slips an errant tomato into my carry-out.

I just wonder if I might be missing out on some other tomatoes in my world that I've decided are nasty and slimy and full of seeds. Wouldn't it be a shame if I got to the end of my life and realized I'd been missing out on a great delicacy?

Dear God:
Don't you think Attorneys General is an awkward term?

You know what I'm talking about. One Attorney General files a law-suit against an industry or company with a great deal of money that's been earned from harming his beloved public in some way. Then, the Attorney General in the state next door and on the other coast and so forth join in the fray. We go from Attorney General to Attorneys General. It's a term that would never have been used more often than at the annual Attorneys General Convention if it weren't for the tobacco companies, gunmakers, Microsoft, and class-action lawsuits.

That's a funny-sounding term, don't you think? I had to hear it five or six times on radio newscasts to grasp that the plural part of the term goes in the first word instead of the last. I went through all the logic. "O.K., they must be attorneys first before they can become an Attorney General." Is that why we say it that way? Or, is it just a term someone conjured up to sound sophisticated?

Why couldn't they have been attorney generals. Does that sound too military? Couldn't we have called them Secretary of Law? How about Secretary of Justice? That has a majestic ring.

You're right; Why should I care why they're called attorneys general in the plural form? The fact is, I wouldn't much care if they hadn't become so active in the last few years, and I had to hear about the brave new steps they're taking to seek recompense for every harmful product man has devised.

I suppose the reason I wondered about this benign term has more to do with the work I see happening on the part of Attorneys General throughout the land. This fine group of chief law enforcement personnel have joined their *juris doctor* associates in elevating the art of legal action in this country to a new prominence. They don't get one-third of the settlement, but they're certainly acting like the increasingly rich arbitrators who have become such familiar figures in our modern culture.

Did our propensity to sue one another and the recognition that comes from big settlements encourage Attorneys General to jump in the fray, or are these modern crusaders bent on righting the wrongs that unchecked big business perpetrates on society? Are Attorneys General the odd cousins of other seekers of social justice, or are they opportunists who know the Governor's office is a great next stop for a champion of the people?

I wouldn't mention the cynical side of this equation were it not for the waiting game that I've seen played by a few. "I haven't decided if it will be in our state's best interest to join this class action suit. I'll wait until the facts become clear on what is in the best interest of the people of (insert state) before making a decision." This approach happens a little too often for my comfort. To me, that often translates, "I need to be sure this is winnable and that people support this particular action before sticking my neck out."

Yes, I'm cynical about this type of behavior, but I've seen enough to know that what someone says and what he means aren't always exactly the same thing. I like to lay the blame on people in elected office for this kind of behavior. I realize their behavior isn't much different from people in business, except that their words are played out in every newscast and every publication. I also recognize that I've said disingenuous things to people more than a couple of times to keep from making a commitment.

Is it difficult to be a crusader and maintain good intentions? Does intent matter as long as the job is done? You know it matters to me. As an idealist, I struggle with the give and take of dirtying my hands to complete a job. After all, it's much easier to throw rocks at people who appear to sell their souls for the chance at fame. I've tossed some rocks in their direction.

I wonder if I'm not being too hard on someone who sought an office I'd never seek and to do a job I'd never want to do. I wonder if the world doesn't need people who will bridge the gap between the less tasteful side of life and the side of human good.

As I recall, the Bible instructs Christians "to be in this world, but not of it." That's a very difficult distinction to make. Those who are serious about their faith would find it very easy to punt. "Not my problem to deal with those scalliwags," they might say. "God will even the books on them before it's over and done. If not, they'll kill each other off." History says that in this life you might, and you might not, at least to human understanding.

We've seen the opposite of that approach, too; We've seen committed Christians who become part of the power structure to attempt change. In the end, they're often the ones who are changed, resulting to the same devious tactics they deplore from those who don't believe.

Those two opposites leave the rest of us who fall somewhere in the middle in a state of limbo. Should we voice our opinions? Or should we love our enemies into submission? Or should we jump on the bandwagon when something is so very wrong that to stay silent makes us as guilty as the people committing the egregious act? How do we know the right time to speak up?

Should our time be spent feeding the hungry, clothing the naked, visiting those in prison? Or, are we supposed to be activists for change at a political level? In other words, is there a difference between a politician who goes to church because it makes for good political mileage and a Christian who jumps into politics because the church hasn't been effective in influencing the lives of enough people to bring society back to you?

If you could be an attorney general for a day, would you join in the class-action lawsuit mania, or would you look for ways to change people so that their behaviors didn't become the problems of state? In this country there are fifty attorneys general, along with fifty governors and a number of lieutenant governors and several thousand legislators. Which is the most important part of their job: to pick between warring opinions or to act in good conscience? How would you choose?

As you know, I've had the opportunity lately to gain a better understanding of the factors that influence the life of a child over the long-term. One of those factors is education. I've learned that it costs over $16,000 a year for the state of South Carolina to keep one person in prison. The school district here spends a little over $5,000 per year per student. It's been noted that more than 50% of prisoners are functionally illiterate and that many at-risk children in our world have parents whose own lack of education prevents them from providing assistance to their children with basic elementary school homework.

If we could reduce the number of people in prison, we could spend more to ensure that the children of people imprisoned by their lack of education don't repeat the cycle, at a much lower cost and at a much greater benefit to society. It's easier to lock people up and ignore the problems they've left behind than it is to find a solution for that most basic predictor of society's future direction: a child.

You see how tough the choices are? We want people to be accountable for their actions, but we lack the grace to ensure their offspring don't suffer the same fate.

If anybody's in it for the long run, it's certainly you. Could you help us understand how to make good choices with nasty issues? Many people have already decided what your answer is. I'd like to hear some confirmation from you.

Whether we're attorneys or generals or everyday citizens, all of us need the wisdom you can bring to the issues that divide us so.

Dear God:
Are you still a member in good standing at Augusta National?

I suppose that's a silly question. Not that you wouldn't have an opportunity to move among the chosen, but that there's any such thing as a member who's not in good standing. There are only two types of people in the world: members in good standing at Augusta and the rest of us.

If there ever was a modern-day Eden, it would have to be Augusta National Golf Club. Nowhere on earth does the harmony of perfected nature combine with such genteel graciousness. The starkness of a mountain range, the babble of a mountain brook, the rush of the ocean onto a beach. All beautiful, but none as classically sculpted as that one plot of land during the second week of April.

I've been happy to be an interloper on seven or eight occasions in my life, and never have I felt more grateful for an opportunity to be in such an exclusive place. I've been to big-time sporting events, and, after most of them, I've felt that aside from being able to say I was there, it would have been better to watch on television. Not The Masters. Never have I felt the afterglow of a sporting event as I have after a day at Augusta.

I've watched The Masters on television numerous times. As you'll remember, one Sunday in 1986 I was reduced to wiping tears from my eyes as Jack Nicklaus made his miraculous march around the back nine. I'm not sure if my tears were for the miracle of the Golden Bear's late charge, or with regret that I wasn't there in person to see it.

Augusta has always been an almost sacred place for a golfer and a very tightly run ship as well. When I last went, it was a place for very golf-like behavior. Upon walking in, the feeling arose that I had entered golf's holy of holies. One wore golf shoes to Augusta. For the non-golfers who weaseled their way in, tennis shoes were acceptable, but garish.

If anyone forgot that Augusta represented the genteel nature of golf during their stay, they generally had the chance to watch the remainder of the event on television with the owner of the pass likely to be dismissed from further subscription to what has long been regarded the toughest ticket in sports.

But that's been more than a decade ago. I understand much has changed. I wonder if you could confirm my suspicions about what has happened since my last trip. No one offers me tickets any more. The people that used to offer me tickets are still around, but they don't seem to be in line for someone's spares. If they are, they aren't giving them to me. Granted, it was usually ten p.m. the night before when I heard from them, but some things are worth changing plans over. It's never bothered me one bit to be on someone's <u>C</u> or <u>D</u> list. As people say after someone makes the ugliest par in history, "It still says four on the scorecard."

The first thing I've understood from others is that tickets are getting more expensive. I'm not talking about what those on the ticket list pay for the tickets though I imagine inflation has taken its toll. I'm talking about what, let's call them resellers, are getting for the tickets. When I attended, I never paid for a single ticket. I'm not sure many other people did, either. Tickets to The Masters were a gift given to someone as a token of friendship or to signify his importance as a customer, sort of like the special-order hams some people give their best customers for Christmas. You could receive them, but you couldn't buy them.

I've heard there are tickets for sale these days; I hear those tickets are very, very expensive. It used to be that anyone could show up for a practice round, pay his ten bucks at the gate, and go in. I understand those days are gone as well.

I suspect what's happened to The Masters is the same thing that's happened to society in general. I'm not talking about supply and demand. Given the relatively small number of tickets issued for the tournament, demand has always outstripped supply. I think those tickets couldn't be bought, or most of them anyway so demand had more to do with having the right friends or the right connection than it did with having a fat money clip.

Masters tickets have fallen prey to the American need to seek status through inclusion in big-name events. There are now people who are willing to travel from all over to attend The Masters. People who have access to the tickets have found these event voyagers are willing to pay big bucks for the honor of being in attendance. The American way has taken over.

It doesn't matter anymore if someone is a racing fan, you have to go to Indy. It doesn't matter if you've never seen a horse, you must do the Kentucky Derby. We've become a society that's increasingly obsessed at being in the all the right places. Memories used to be created on front porches. Now, they're weekend snapshots for the family scrapbook. It used to be that a family vacation to the Grand Canyon would turn up as a snoozer of a slide show or grainy film on a projector. Now, it's a Glamor Shots package purchased through an entrepreneur who's making big money from someone else's big money.

So it has become with The Masters. Or, so it appears to me. I'm sure The Masters controls what is offered and purchased inside its gates with the same fervor as past days, but I'm afraid the control outside the gates isn't what it once was. The price of seeing and being seen has gone up.

Oddly, The Masters was an exclusive enclave where the price of concessions was surprisingly low considering the surroundings and the limit on tickets. But then, the tournament wasn't about money. Most people who played in it would have played for nothing except the chance to wear the green jacket. Maybe they still will. Is The Masters an example of something that can keep the turmoil outside its gates for only so long? The times they are a'changing.

From what I can tell, Augusta is no longer the sanctuary of a mostly Southern, generally upscale crowd. It has become a national tournament where the seats go to the highest bidder. I'm sure many still cling grimly to their tickets, bestowing them only as favors, but it's obvious from some things I've heard and observed that money has won the day if admittance to the tournament is the goal.

I don't think the wholesale "brokering" of tickets is good, but then no one's offered me any free tickets lately. But it's also obvious that money now drives the show more than anyone who loves the tournament would care to admit.

Is Augusta National a modern-day example of what happened to the Garden of Eden? Are the pure motives of someone who fought to keep his amateur status now being gradually eroded by the success of the place he created? Have the current crowds, much like sin creeping into the garden, forgotten the sanctity of this neatly clipped paradise?

As I watched the broadcast of today's final round, I couldn't help but notice the difference as the final twosome walked up the sixteenth fairway. Vijay Singh, a fine golfer with a PGA title and a dignified air under his belt, received the steady wash of applause from the crowd as he made his way toward the green. Only at Augusta does the applause reach a restrained but moving crescendo, as the apparent champion to be makes his way up the sixteenth fairway.

He held a three-stroke lead with two holes and two putts to play. His closest rival for most of the day, David Duval, watched his opportunity to catch Singh splash away on an errant second shot at the thirteenth hole. Singh walked in front, with Duval behind. Singh had a long but two-puttable par in his grasp.

Duval had a shorter but still difficult putt for birdie to bring him within two strokes.

You saw what happened. Singh left a long putt for par. Duval narrowly missed a birdie. Singh then missed the par putt, leaving only two strokes between him and Duval. From the crowd, several voices shouted out, "Come on, David." At Augusta, that's unthinkable. Or, it used to be. The game's purity eroding away in a wash of favoritism. And yet, the azaleas and dogwoods were just as beautiful, and the grass perfect beyond compare.

Was it like this in the Jack and Arnie days? Nobody liked Jack back then, but did the crowds openly pull for Arnie? I wasn't old enough to know, but I bet not.

The scary part to me isn't that some invaders did the shouting. The scary part is that the people who did the shouting might have held tickets for years and have now forgotten the sanctity of the place.

Have we come to the point where nothing is sacred? Has the outside world finally reached inside this golfing Eden?

Maybe you're still a member in good standing. For all the marvels of man-made splendor, none of it would be worth much without the azaleas and dogwoods, the blue sky of a perfect April day, and the wash of late-afternoon sunlight through the Georgia pines. If you are, perhaps you could help us see the sanctity of this place for golf.

Perhaps you'll further help us understand that the sanctity of some of your other best work is a cause for both hushed reverence and a steady crescendo of appreciative applause.

Dear God:
Is "professional casual" an oxymoron?

I hope you're not wearing whatever your version of a golf shirt might be at this moment, but I've paused to think lately that the standards of dress that I so enjoy every working day might not be that good for me. I don't want to go back to wearing a suit to work. I hate to put one on for the occasional client or for the all too frequent funeral, but I've begun to wonder if that oxymoronic term, "professional casual," might be a telling symptom of a bigger disease.

I probably wouldn't have given this much thought, aside from those two times a year when sweaters and golf shirts are at their clearance-price lows, had it not been for an Internet news article I saw this week about acceptable standards of "professional casual" dress. The article included a picture of a woman wearing a dress, still not that unusual. This dress, however, had oval openings all the way around the waist, like a skin-belt of some sort. Perhaps with some people's reluctance to wear animal skins, human skin for a belt is considered a proper substitute. But does it have any place in the office?

I don't know what the article said because I didn't finish it. It's not that I wasn't interested in what conclusions the article might draw, but the web page wouldn't open to the full story, one of the hazards of Internet links. Though I don't know to which

115

side the writer's opinion fell, I drew a quick conclusion of my own. I think I'd be paying a great deal more attention to the human skin belt than the animal substitute.

The other thing that interested and amused me about the article was the fact that there *was* an article on the subject. The need to explore the fundamentals of such a topic felt the same as if my third grade teacher had sent me a note when I got my first job explaining that, when your nose is running, it's generally considered good taste to use a tissue or a handkerchief.

Nonetheless, this article started me thinking about professional casual dress and the changing times. Before I could afford more than one really nice suit, the challenge was to find a mix and match of pants and shirts and ties that would make me look presentable. I also remember in those days that I was a little envious, and a little intimidated, by people who had climbed far enough up the ladder to be able to afford big-time suits.

Professional casual is a more equitable way to dress though a $90 golf shirt is noticeably different from the $30 variety. The saving grace of my place of employment is that it's full of engineers. For most engineers, clothes are something you have to wear to be able to go to work in the morning without getting arrested.

There are a few non-engineers and a few deviant engineers in the building, and professional casual is an opportunity to show your stuff. At our place, it's generally tasteful. For the old hands, it has meant they quit wearing ties but kept wearing dress pants and dress shirts with the top button open. For the middle-aged among us, it's translated into golf shirts, golf vests, and sweaters. We're a conservative bunch, so there haven't been any women running around with see-through belts on though cleavage has peeked its way in. I haven't heard anyone complaining.

What I'm really wondering about this whole professional casual business is what it has done to people's attitudes about work. Is work now more productive since the male employees don't risk being asphyxiated by their ties? Do people have more energy from not wearing around an extra five pounds of clothes? Or is it that professional casual is simply a way to take one small bit of strain from people's lives when they get up in the morning?

You and I have talked about the change in attitudes of people in general over the last decade, the last five years in particular. Maybe professional casual is an expression of societal change. Yep, even I'm smart enough to figure that out. But I wonder if it isn't more significant.

Could it be that the fluid nature of employment situations these days make people less loyal? Do no more contracts for life or the lack of status or even employment based on tenure make people care less?

Even the individuality that can be expressed through professional casual dress doesn't explain the change in attitudes. It's a symptom, not the disease.

I think professional casual represents a lack of discipline that once existed, no matter how smothering it might have been in some circumstances. There was a day when everyone rallied around the company banner, made the sacrifices necessary to get the job done, and were more willing to be inspired by the leadership of the organization.

I've found of late that more people than ever see work as something they have to get through so that they can get paid and spend precious time doing things they think will make them happy. Have you noticed that people don't seem to work as hard anymore?

I'm sure there are many examples out there of people working seventy-hour weeks on a regular basis, but I have a sense that it's not happening in as widespread a manner as it once did. Perhaps people are working the same number of hours, but complaining more about it.

People may have been abused enough by the lack of loyalty our modern world promotes to not care more than they need to just live. Perhaps they're finding that there's more to life than just work. I have a feeling that, deep down inside, we would all have more enthusiasm for work, regardless of the dress code, if we felt it had worth beyond a paycheck.

I think people are just tired. Professional casual is a way to make them feel less tired than they are. I also think professional casual can contribute to a lack of caring, whatever the cause.

Do you see life as casual or professional? Does filling our souls from your deep reserve require that we dress the part on occasion? Do our souls need a suit and tie to truly reflect on the deeper issues of our relationship with you?

At times, I miss the days of having to dress the part. I don't miss it enough to want to go back to it, but I think I might have seen work as a more worthy part of my life then.

I wonder if our relationship with you doesn't have that same element. Are we more casual about our relationship with you because, in the long run, nothing seems permanent anymore?

Dear God:
What has a longer lifespan,
a dot-com company
or a dragonfly?

I'm looking for a quick, sweet deal. As usual, my timing is awful. It looks as though all those great internet-related companies are finally having to deal with reality. Just when I thought I'd stumble across the next sleeping giant, it looks as though the spending spree is over. I'm not a bit richer than I was when this insanity started. Of course, I'm not any poorer either.

Last week I read that most dragonflies have a life span of perhaps one month. Certainly, that's shorter than the life span of the once high-flying dot-com companies, but the dragonfly holds an advantage. The dragonfly produces more dragonflies, and they buzz around for a while carrying out dragonfly functions. In short time, there are new dragonflies. And on it goes. Dragonflies, though their individual lives are short, have an endearing permanence about them.

I'm no expert in the market. I've speculated in very small amounts of money and made more than I lost. I'm at least $500 to the good. I finally turned over what little I have to a mutual fund, and it seems to be growing fairly steadily, but I have absolutely no idea where these money managers are putting my money. Perhaps I don't want to know.

When I was much younger, I thought I would hit a great deal and make a million from a $10,000 investment. But through experience, I learned that the risks were just as high as the reward, and perhaps consistent investing made more sense than looking for one fat deal.

This tech stock race got my juices flowing, and I started paying attention again, thinking I'd find that magical stock where one hit would generate financial returns beyond my wildest dreams. I was too late for Yahoo, Amazon, Cisco, AOL and all the others. Doubling my money wasn't enough. There were people making gains in thousands of percentage points. All I had to do was find the right one.

I still hoped for another promising but obscure number to stick its head up so that only I could see it. What happened instead, is that the false bottom holding up the value of all these profitless good ideas fell out and with it the future of companies that didn't exist two years ago and won't exist by next year.

The point is that I wanted some instant gratification for very little effort, like many other folks it seems. I was looking for that one opportunity to make the American dream my reality. Now we've talked, or at least I've talked to you, about what I'd do if I had a lot of money. I know you haven't forgotten that I intend to put as much of these spoils as possible under federal tax laws to good use. Perhaps it's likely to remain a dream, a very distracting dream I might add. Which leads to the question of investing in your eyes. Do you want me to pay more attention to dragonflies? I recall that Jesus pointed to the birds and noted they neither reaped nor sowed, yet they never lacked for what they needed. It has also been pointed out that birds have to do some flying to be fed.

Still, I recognize that I have far more materially than 99% of the people on the face of the earth, but that's not enough sometimes when you have a clear view of the other 1%.

Since dragonflies are pretty small, I don't imagine their brains are large enough to do a whole lot of processing. Yet they seem to manage as long as they stay away from pond surfaces with a hungry fish directly underneath.

There's something to be learned from a dragonfly's life, isn't there? In your plan, there's an insect we call a dragonfly that serves a purpose. In the case of the dragonfly, that plan includes keeping the mosquito population down. Everything serves some purpose, except apparently some of the dot-com ideas. In the natural order of your world, so do dragonflies. That leads me to the natural conclusion that I'm here to serve a purpose, and, apparently, that purpose isn't to be filthy rich.

Dragonflies are fairly singular in purpose, and I assume in their focus. Humans, on the other hand, have many options as to what their purpose is, and many distractions that get in the way of focusing on that purpose. I don't suppose dragonflies have addictions or identity crises. I can't imagine dragonflies having financial difficulty since closing a loan would take longer than their short existence.

You made us the crowning glory of your creation, and you, no doubt, expect us to produce more. By now you've realized the flip side is we'll be more trouble as well.

What made me think of all these things is Easter. As you're well aware, it's Easter today. And as you're also aware, I made my way to Your House this morning for the celebration. And it was a celebration. I felt that. Thank you.

During the course of the sermon, the pastor, a wise man, spent some time talking about the enduring nature of Jesus. He discussed the difference between myth and reality. He talked about Jesus' death as a historical fact, not as an abstraction or a myth. I got it.

I began to think of permanence from your standpoint. In Jesus' day, he looked like a flash-in-the-pan to the people who watched him put to death. He had three years of ministry, about the life span of a dot-com company apparently.

Yet, his life has endured all these years and appears to be in for a good showing in the new millennium as well. Of course, his was a profound life to say the least—a one-time occurrence that achieved exactly what you intended to achieve, or at least set in place what you knew had to be in place if there were any long-term hope for the rest of us.

Your type of permanence is so different from ours. Maybe that's why we have such a hard time connecting with you. We want what we want when we want it. You, on the other hand, look at the dragonflies and us, and you see the dragonflies droning around in their purposeful little ways, and you see us wandering about trying to find any purpose at all, and you let us both keep doing what we're doing.

What's the lesson of Jesus when it comes to purpose? He preached a spiritual kingdom, a kingdom with an unlimited life span. When it comes to my relative affluence and the affluence of the society around me, that type of kingdom is hard to grasp because it doesn't have any brand names on it.

The little consumer we're raising understands the significance of brand quite well. Fortunately, he also has a good understanding of the significance of the kingdom taught by Jesus. Some days I think he understands it better than his parents.

How do I find this spiritual kingdom in the midst of all this short-term focus? I've looked around of late and noticed that, with all the wealth that exists, there's no limit to what we could do as a country to bring those most disadvantaged among us up the ladder a bit. But it takes a long-time to deal with something like that, and, when you can double your money on speculation in six months, why invest in something as predictably grim as the vicious cycle of a child from a background of poverty and ignorance?

Maybe the answer is to break another cycle, the cycle of short-term reward. I might be looking at things the wrong way in my haste to get what's mine. But, as you know, I'll need some help there. I've learned to live one way, and it has twisted my perspective more than I'd like to consider.

If you have any ideas on improving on my investment schemes, feel free to let me know. I just might be in a mood to listen.

Dear God:
Which came first, stupidity, or call-in radio talk shows?

If I ever want a fresh reminder of why the human race has so many problems, all I have to do is turn on the radio to a call-in talk show. I know you see all of the stories and attitudes that turn up on talk radio before they ever hit the airwaves, so I suppose you're used to it, but I've never been close enough, long enough, to the level of thinking that generally appears from the callers and the hosts of these types of shows to listen without my temperature rising.

Yes, I know it's entertainment, but I wish they'd call it that and quit dressing it up as some attempt to address real issues. As far as I can tell, the only real issue that's been resolved for certain is the confirmation that 99 percent of the country apparently has a complete lack of curiosity about any viewpoint other than their own. It's rare that someone calling in begins with, "You know, I had something to say, but after listening to that other fellow, I've changed my mind."

As a matter of fact, I've reached the startling conclusion that call-in shows are about getting people to take sides. Yes, I know that's a blinding glimpse of the obvious, but I'm not sure most people are getting it. Of course, to take sides, it generally helps to have a provocateur leaning heavily to one side or the other serving as the host.

Two magic words, God. Two magic words control call-in shows of the political variety anyway. Liberal and conservative, or to be balanced, conservative and liberal. What's really spooky about this label-on-demand approach to any opinion that differs from whomever has the phone line or the microphone at that point in time, is how quickly people have learned the conservative and liberal buzz words. They don't understand much else, but they've learned how to spot a liberal lurking behind a government program or a conservative peeking from behind a tax cut. Those basic ideas are the content of these shows. Liberals are for big government and conservatives are for less government. Don't let the record show that politicians spend money in copious amounts, but on different things, based on their political affiliation.

And that's where we are today; choosing sides over things that aren't going to make much difference in the long run. Don't let anyone know that most of the agendas bandied about in talk-land are fine theory, and that's about it. The real world does what it's going to do while these folks are talking and it's generally not truly conservative or truly liberal; it's just what needed to be done to keep things moving.

I can't help but wonder how much could get done if we quit worrying about labels and started actually thinking about how to bring people together. I suspect these solutions would be somewhere in the middle, but don't tell anybody that or you'll never attract enough enthusiasm for your agenda either.

But then again, maybe the answers aren't in the middle. Maybe the answers are both conservative and liberal. Maybe the answers lie in line with the wisdom of the Bible. We like selecting passages that in and of themselves push a specific point of view. Perhaps if we looked at the total sweep of the Bible and your relationship to man, we would get a different perspective.

There's discipline and forgiveness. There's love with a firm hand. There's an understanding that different people from different backgrounds have different ways of doing things. I seem to remember that the wise men came from a great distance, while the locals had no room at the inn.

The Bible also provides the understanding that your standard for everyone is the same, whether we're victims of society or not. But it also points to a Savior who took society's refuse and paid attention to it.

But you already know all that. Let's revisit our call-in show hosts for a minute, if you don't mind. What really boils me is the tone that has apparently become *de rigeur* today. Whether it's right Ron or lefty Lou, they've all taken on a form of arrogance that makes me feel physically ill. I didn't realize you had so many prophets out there with diametrically opposed points of view. But that's what society has become: people trying to shout loudly enough to be heard over the noise of everyone else who has something to say but not much in the way of motivation to make any actual changes.

To make it worse, some of the hosts actually sound angry. I don't know if the anger is feigned or real, but in either case, I don't think it's fitting for someone trying to conduct a discourse on issues to get all self-righteous about it. If the anger is real, people are speaking from some well of bitterness that shouldn't be foisted on everyone else. If the anger is part of the show, some of these experts on fixing all the ills of society should be smart enough to realize they're stirring up people who have decided not to think for themselves, which is exactly what they intended.

And that makes me angry. And it has made me almost angry enough to pick up the phone and call in, which just proves they're working their magic with me, too.

The only decent talk show I've heard lately was one I caught one night coming through North Carolina. Of all things, it was the high sheriff of a county on a call-in show with two of his prisoners. I couldn't tell if it was being done tongue-in-cheek or if it was supposed to be serious. Either way, it was hilarious in the way that the ridiculous side of human tragedy can be funny. The sheriff railed against all the liberals in Raleigh who didn't want to put people in jail, and the prisoners, both repeat offenders for a variety of offenses, kept getting tripped up on what story they were sticking to that particular evening.

One prisoner, in response to a question about his substance-abuse habits and how it affected his children, said that when he smoked dope he went into a back room of his house so his children couldn't see. The sheriff then had the opportunity to tell the prisoner that if he was still smoking dope, he'd have his deputies busting down the door to his house pretty soon. The prisoner recanted, saying his backroom tokes happened when he *used* to partake, since he was now clean and only waiting for his DWI sentence to be complete before returning home.

Of course the sheriff, knowing this fellow's likely addicted for life, and realizing that he'd see this fellow sooner than later without going over to his house, never made this threat until a caller began talking about how stupid the prisoner was for saying something like that on the air, and in front of the sheriff. It made for fine dramatics and underscored how many people who are now in jail never had enough education to even lie correctly.

Now that's a talk show with two points of view. Yes, the questions the sheriff asked were leading, and yes, no one expected either prisoner to give an eloquent account of himself, but I thought aside from the points the sheriff was trying to score with the electorate, the show had a genuineness about it you just don't hear any more. It pointed out the stark difference between how twisted someone's life can become because of their weaknesses, and the power that's vested in the person who owns them while they're repaying society. It was an honest look at two extremes of our society. Whose side were you on in that particular forum?

I hope you were on both sides, because I have a criminal streak in me. I just haven't gotten caught yet. Nor for the most part have the rest of the people on earth. You couldn't build enough prisons to make all of us account for our poor choices and lack of strength. There wouldn't be enough space in heaven to build enough cells to hold all of us guilty of crimes of the heart.

One other thing about these call-in shows seems worth mentioning. I've noticed that almost everyone that calls begins by asking the host "how are you?", sometimes followed by "love your show." I've noticed that most of the hosts respond with barely concealed contempt. They say "fine" and "glad you enjoy it", but they might as well be saying, "you're standing on my foot" from the vibes I pick up.

Is that something like me saying, "Dear God" followed by "love your creation?" I hope not. I'd hate to think you're listening to me with barely concealed contempt for my needs.

I wonder if people who call these broadcasts think they're making a difference, or are they just blowing off steam? I wonder how much credibility they give these self-proclaimed experts. And I wonder how much difference it would make if they were seeking some direction from you about some of the issues we always have answers for but rarely get around to solving.

Dear God:
How is Eleanor Rigby doing?

Since The Beatles carried her story throughout the music universe in 1966, we haven't heard much of Eleanor Rigby, except in 2:05 repeats of the song that made her name a household item. I wondered how she's doing now that the bonds of her lonely existence among us no longer hold her. Does she know how big her name became in death? Millions now recognize her name though few knew she existed while she was alive.

Funny thing about her life, God. She only lived for one verse. One short verse:
"Eleanor Rigby picks up the rice in a church
where a wedding has been.
Lives in a dream.
Waits at the window, wearing a face that
she keeps in a jar by the door.
Who is it for?
All the lonely people, where do they all come from?
All the lonely people, where do they all belong?"

Where *do* all the lonely people come from? Who are they? I'm sure I see them every day, but they're generally not talking, because loneliness must be one of the hardest needs to describe to another person. The times when I felt loneliest in my life were also times I couldn't tell anybody how lonely I was, because it made me look weak and foolish, and, let's face it, alone. Loneliness means that we're not worthy of having companionship or love. I can't imagine someone spilling the beans to someone else about being lonely. It's a vicious cycle isn't it?

Lonely people are all around, aren't they? They're all around, and I don't know who they are. Most days I don't care a great deal about who they are because fixing someone's loneliness means being involved in their life in some way, and that's asking a lot. Wouldn't you have to know someone pretty well to know if that person is lonely or not?

Are there clues? Is it a distant expression in the middle of a full-strength social gathering? Is it listening but not joining in to the Monday morning chatter about what we all did over the weekend? Is it deferring personal questions when someone gets too close for comfort? Or is that just being private?

I'm sure you hear from lots of lonely people. And I bet some of them are the life of any party. They're the life of the party because without that superficial interaction, they'd have no interaction at all. I bet you're the only source for pouring out their loneliness. But, I bet even with you the L word probably doesn't surface very often. Loneliness is masked by so many other symptoms that we never get around to the real problem.

If you asked me for an image of a lonely person, I'd recall an a television public service campaign showing an older woman sitting by a window watching the world go by, but loneliness is more than people who spend most of their time alone.

I remember times I could admit my loneliness to myself, but certainly not to anyone else. What I remember most about it was the sadness in realizing that I had no one, at that time, who was part of me. I know that so many of the things I've done in my life that weren't wise were a counter to loneliness. All the time I was surrounded by people and doing things with people and dropping further and further into a hole of loneliness because none of it actually meant anything. I was just pushing time forward.

I've also felt the loneliness of being the center of attention. Sometimes loneliness means being singled out, even if it is for praise, because distance has been put between us and the people around us that didn't exist before. In that sense, you must feel lonely at times, too.

Loneliness is a very ugly thing. It's the opposite of companionship. It's the opposite of deep interaction. It's the opposite of loving and being loved.

I also remember the times when I was content, but I wasn't spending a lot of time seeking the company of other people. I wasn't lonely then. I was fulfilled with who I was, and if I remember correctly, I was also content in my fulfillment through and with you.

You made us to be together, to lean on each other, to see your likeness in each person with whom we come in contact. Yet, we have such a difficult time getting around to actually seeing someone for who they really are. We treat relationships like transactions. Figure out what you want and then act in the way that's required to get it.

Yet, the truest relationships I've seen came from expecting nothing but the trust and companionship of another human being. And those glimpses of true relationship make loneliness even uglier than if we never glimpsed true relationship at all.

For one thing, going to that kind of effort is risky business. We might just run into someone we wish we hadn't met. Life's risky. But I wonder if playing it safe is better than living in a shell of loneliness. I wonder if playing it safe is better than never knowing what true relationships can do to raise the quality of life. I wonder if playing it safe is better than venturing out into the world and scraping our knees and bumping our heads to find out what marvelous curiosities await us. Are the lonely people of the world the ones who can't or won't take those chances?

I wonder how it would feel if we were in better contact with you. Distance is perceived more often that it's actual. We tend to think something or someone is a long way away if we don't like the time or effort it's going to take to get closer to our destination. Some days you seem like a short drive. Some days it seems like you're in the deepest part of South Georgia, which from here takes five or six hours that seem like a week.

Some days you're like my eighty-year old neighbor who has some caustic but smile-producing thing to say that makes me appreciate the beauty of growing old and wise. He gives me an insight into his soul that I don't often encounter from people in my daily tasks. I feel warmed by the love and grace and humor he's gained over his four-score years.

But some days you're like the person who won't return my phone calls and keeps me way past arm's length when I show up in person.

The days I can't find you at all are often the days when I need you the most. I have to admit that on the days I don't need you very much, I'm generally not looking as hard. But I've gotten used to an earthly father and mother who respond anytime I call them, whether I've called them seven days in a row before that or not.

Yet, I think you're the answer. I'm betting on it. I can't imagine another answer that's sufficient. I don't want to meditate. I've seen my inner self and it's just a more complicated version of my outer self. I don't want hordes of people seeking to fix what ails me. I think I'm better equipped than just about all of them. I recognize a void that I don't think another person can completely fill. I think it's your space.

There are many people out there like me, God. Their loneliness, whether total or sporadic, is because of you. Some of them know it. Some of them don't. The ones who know it are waiting for a calming reassurance that you're around. The others just know there's a big chunk of something missing that they can't find in anything physical. And I'm afraid there's a larger group who don't want to consider they might be missing anything at all.

Even though we're not characters in a song, just remember that the rest of us have a touch of Eleanor Rigby somewhere deep inside. "All the lonely people" come from all over, and, at some time or the other, I suspect it's most of us. If you could help us see your image in other people, perhaps we wouldn't feel so far from you. Perhaps we'd see the glory of creation shining from another set of human eyes.

Dear God:
Did you hear the one about the rabbi, the priest, and the Baptist minister?

Actually, I've heard several humorous variations on that theme. I'm sure you have, too. I think the last one I heard involved a round of golf, or maybe that one was about you, Moses, and Jesus on the links. Anyway, there are as many variations out there as there are religious denominations.

I don't bring up the question to ask you what you find amusing about the eccentricities of our different ways of trying to find you, which we call religions or faiths. I asked because I've begun to wonder more and more where you stand on the issue of religious practice. Not faith, but religious practice.

I just wonder where you stand. All of us, whether we're Catholic or Jewish or Baptist or some sect of Uncle Festus look-alikes, tend to think it's our way or the highway. Even the Unitarian Universalists must not think the rest of us are right, or they'd be one of us. See the logic of all this?

I wonder which of us is right. To be even more direct, I wonder if any of us have it all right. Perhaps I should ask if any of us have some of it right. Come to think of it, that may be the UU's whole point.

A partial reason I'm asking this question is that fewer and fewer people feel the need to cast their lot on a regular basis with any religious organization these days. Oh, there's plenty of movement from church to church and from denomination to denomination by those who have either been taught that going to church is a good thing or by those actually seeking a relationship with you. You know the difference much better than I as to who fits into what category. In fact, I'm afraid you know which category I fit better than I do.

Another reason I'm curious is because it seems that identifying with a specific church or a denomination tends to lead people to discount the religious experience of others. Those who aren't Baptists or some close relative, generally see us Baptists as a bunch of ignorant hicks who are hung up on dancin' and drinkin' and other sins of the flesh. They may be right, but I think that's a bit of a generalization. Baptists and their cousins, on the other hand, tend to see the less evangelical organizations out there as being too wishy-washy, and probably not worth taking seriously.

I bring this to your attention because you're the cause of this dissension. Yep, all this dissension is about you. We would rather fight about you than find meaning in you. If you weren't around, our rivalries would center on whether the Lions or the Rotary or the Optimists or the Sertoma were the best service organization. But since you are around, we've built at least two millennia of religious practice in trying to define who you are, how we're supposed to find you, and what you want us to do.

Everyone has the answer, except that all their answers are somewhat different. Sometimes the differences are substantive, and sometimes they're a matter of practice rather than belief.

For example, some denominations that don't see much differently otherwise, differ over the practice of baptism. There are the sprinklers and the dunkers. There are the take-it-to-a-body of fresh water baptizers and the in-ground pool, otherwise known as a baptistry, baptizers. Perhaps what we need to further diversify baptismal practices are the 10-meter board baptizers who must select a dive with a difficulty factor of at least 5.0 as a true show of faith. I suspect that would get everyone's attention for a while, if for no other reason than to see if there's a Russian judge in the congregation to give it a low score.

I had never given much thought to any of this until a few years back. The reason it became a matter of importance then was two-fold. For one, I began to take my faith, which includes religious practice, much more seriously. And two, the denomination I was born into began to take itself pretty seriously as well. As a matter of fact, it began to take itself so seriously that I had trouble taking it seriously.

I began to think about what I believed and why I believed it. I found that much of what I believed had been passed down to me by my parents, and by well-meaning Sunday School teachers and pastors and such. For the most part, I'd taken what they said, and said to myself, "OK".

I've learned, as I've grown older, that life is very complex. It raises all sorts of questions that don't have easy answers, or any answers at all. What I began to hear, once I started paying attention, is that most religions think they must have answers to all of these difficult, and sometimes unanswerable questions. Some of the answers strike me as patently ridiculous.

That's when I began to realize that faith in you and religious practice aren't one and the same. I probably knew it all along, but once my faith became a central part of how my life was lived out, some of the things I'd been told suddenly didn't quite square anymore. Finding you became more important than a style of worship or a carefully honed theological basis.

In this same period of time, you'll remember that we moved to another city for a short time. This move meant finding a church to attend. We received some recommendations from folks in the know and made the rounds. All the churches had some really fine people in them. All the churches had some people in them that I wouldn't want to associate with on a yearly basis, much less weekly.

We went to a couple of Baptist churches, and even a Presbyterian church, so we didn't cover the whole spectrum. But I saw enough to know that people are basically the same.

Seeing the types of people in these churches wasn't what really made me think. What made me think was going somewhere different, and being a stranger to the local scene. I'd listen to the words of a song, or watch the particular ritual that the church used in its services, and think, "What does it mean?"

Not that these rituals were much different in substance from what I grew up with, but somehow, seeing them in a place I didn't know and among people I didn't know, and feeling a bit out of place for all of that, I found observing worship became a disembodying, third-party experience. I might as well have been floating around on the ceiling watching it all, because none of it felt like it was part of me. I don't think it was wrong, nor do I doubt it had some merit. I just didn't get it.

What I finally understood was why people who have never set foot in a church feel that worship is such an odd experience when they do show up one Sunday.

It didn't stop there. When I went back to my own church after all of this, I began to notice how strange our own rituals seemed. I looked at it as if it were new and wondered exactly what it meant to you. Since then, I still don't quite get it, but I've gotten more comfortable. Whether my returning comfort is a good thing or not, I'm unsure. I still have enough discomfort to know there's something missing for me.

I also wonder how much we're missing in our relationship with you if we base our futures on the idiosyncrasies of denominational practice rather than dealing with real issues of faith. I'm sure that I was brought up with as much denominational belief as I was with real matters of faith. Remember, I came up in what people now remember as a golden age, before terrorists and hijackings, before oil embargoes and a public debate over abortion. It was the age when WWII veterans came home, started raising families and created the baby boom.

People didn't question as much in those days. People were joiners, and to be a joiner, you had to subscribe to the organization's beliefs and practices. Today, we aren't joiners. In fact, we're a little suspicious of anything that's organized.

And here I am, stuck in the middle. I'm a suspicious, old-time joiner who wants to get to the essential you without having to go through all the white noise that denominations have tacked on through the years.

I suppose I could practice my faith without being part of any organization. It would certainly save on the strain of dealing with budgets and church personnel and building maintenance and social functions.

But I know and you know there is strength in numbers. My concern is that the people who represent those numbers become the focus at your expense. That's how I see churches these days: a fine idea that's become an instrument of human creature comforts more often than an instrument of you.

One of the answers for some people has been to start and join churches that don't have any denominational label on them, but to me, being non-denominational is a bit of a label in itself.

If there's no getting around it then, this is the type of church I'd like to be in. First of all, it wouldn't own a building and would never own a building. The staff would have jobs other than being a member of the church staff. All of the money except a very small percentage needed for basic expenses would go to ministry that reached out to the world.

Finally, I would like for worship to be very simple. I'd like to find you and contemplate you and your nature. I would like worship to be an act between the two of us.

That's what I want. What kind of church do you want? After all, it is about you.

Dear God:
Do you ever rationalize?

A coworker once told me that we don't go through a day without rationalizing something. It was one of those times when someone said something obviously true that I'd never considered. I sorted through the truth behind his words. It became part of me.

I realized my coworker was right. When I don't want to do something, I convince myself that it can wait, or that it wasn't important in the first place. If I meet someone and we don't hit it off, I surmise what must be wrong with that person not being in tune with me. You know we all rationalize things, more often than not, to keep from taking responsibility. Something was someone else's fault, or the stars weren't lined up correctly, or the dog ate our homework, even though we left it next to his food dish covered in gravy.

When this guy crosses my mind, that one comment pops up. That's it. I believe I worked around him for the better part of two years and that's what I remember; ten seconds of dialogue, and the fact that his hair never made it out of the 70's. I guess that says something about how careful we should be with what we say to other people. They might remember.

What I do know is that from that ten seconds of dialogue, I started looking at my actions, and the actions of those around me, a little bit differently. Oh, you know I still blame other people when I should take responsibility, and you know that I can find a dozen reasons for not doing something I need to do, but I've improved. I improved because of that one simple statement.

I know as God you aren't given to rationalizations, but it seems to me one rationalization may be on your record. And it's a big one: us. Aren't people perhaps your one rationalization?

I'd say think about it, but I'm sure you've had plenty of time and reflection to do just that. But I bet you don't think of our ongoing behavior and your response to it as a rationalization. I bet you think of it as variations in your original plan.

What I'm saying here would cause a lot of people considerable pain—just the mention that we might be a rationalization. In their eyes, I've made you fallible. I don't mean to imply anything of the sort. It's just that from my point of view, it certainly looks as if you dawdled quite a bit in dealing with people. But then, perhaps, I don't understand you at all.

If I could back up for a minute, I'd like to review the sequence of how things came to be. The Bible teaches that you existed when nothing else existed and that you created and ordered the universe to meet your specifications. That's pretty heady stuff. Anyone with the ability to accomplish all of that shouldn't be accused of making a mistake with human beings, the most important element of your work.

What the general sweep of the Bible shows is you coming back to people time and again. You keep giving second chances, and we keep blowing them. You must have known that could or even would happen when you created us. I have to believe you knew there was a chance it could happen. But you carried the plan through understanding the potential for trouble.

Early in the Bible, as in shortly after the creation of Adam and Eve and throughout the remainder of the Old Testament, people continually forgot your gifts and lost sight of your presence. You provided a gentle nudge, and some very firm nudges as well, but your reminders only lasted as long as the memory of hard times last when times are really good.

Giving someone the choice of free will in their decisions is risky business. Yet, you took it.

I can't help but think that you've rationalized a bit. You've made excuses for us, like a guilty parent whose children turned out terribly despite dedicated parental efforts. I can't help but think you've told yourself, "I'll give them more prosperity so they'll understand how much I love them." Or, "Well, yes, they were worshipping that silly golden calf, but it was just foolish fun. I'll give them a slap on the wrist and they'll realize it was wrong. I haven't shown my power enough lately for them to understand."

Or, "I really should let Israel have a King of its own. If I don't, they'll feel inferior to all the countries around them. I just have to find the right man. Then they'll really understand I am looking out for their best interests."

I'm presuming a lot aren't I?

But I have one more example for you. You took your child and sacrificed his life for the good of everyone else. Why take the best and the brightest and bring him to an untimely end? As most anyone knows who can spell Bible, John 3:16 says you did it because you loved the world so much. You lowered yourself that far to show us the way to you.

You rationalized, like any parent, that if you did something so sacrificial and dramatic to prove your love once and for all, we'd fall in line.

But that passage in John also mentions the promise of eternal life. Perhaps what you've ultimately acknowledged is that, while we're on earth in mortal bodies, the odds of us behaving consistently as your children aren't very good. And given our childlike tendency to slip into the cookie jar when we think you aren't looking, maybe you figured out a long time ago that the only way you'll change us is when you give us a new body and start over again.

Or maybe, with the gift of Jesus' life, death and resurrection, you finally decided that if we were going to continually sin, there had to be a way to pass over it without it looking like you'd gone soft. I believe we call that grace.

We should have learned by now. But by and large, we haven't. So, we continue to rebel. Maybe that's why you don't talk directly to many of us anymore—maybe you figure you've let your actions speak louder than words ever could.

Like any child, who realizes upon becoming an adult and a parent, just how trying he must have been for his parents, I'm hoping I can make you proud. I'd hate to think that after all your efforts, you'd be forced to say, "If I'd just given him more wisdom and courage, he'd have recognized how much I cared and wouldn't have fought me so much."

Dear God:
You haven't been watching prices at the pump lately have you?

Things are getting a bit dry here. I'm not talking about oil. It's still flowing. But the volume has been adjusted enough to drive the price of gas higher than it has ever been. There is, however, an even more essential scarcity of a natural product these days over which you have considerable influence.

It's rain, or the lack of it. People who always griped about it raining on a weekend or during a golf game or a sporting event or when they were trying to paint the house, now anxiously hope for dark clouds. Rain has become scarce here.

It's funny how we don't miss the essentials of life until they are in short supply. Now we've learned that with the passing of El Nino and the coming of La Nina, the absence of rain can be as devastating physically and to the spirit as too-much rain. Of course, I live on a hill that would require an ark-building, low-pressure system before there were serious problems, so perhaps I don't find too-much rain as threatening as an area where levees are a basic necessity of life.

I'm also not in the business of producing crops, so my request is purely one of seeing balance returned to nature and hoping my perennials hold on to their title.

Nonetheless, it's dry. With the advent of weather radar from all sorts of online sources, we can constantly tell how dry it is. Those of us who enjoy watching the constant repeats on the Weather Channel will spend hours of fruitless time searching the radar for any greens or yellows or oranges that might be headed our way. Some of us will water twice as much as necessary figuring that if restrictions come, our foliage will survive even if no one else's does.

I'm reminded of a book I read when I was much younger named, *The Year The Yankees Lost the Pennant*. You remember that one, I'm sure. It had the classic elements of good and evil. A middle-aged, fervent fan of the hapless Washington Senators is offered the opportunity to exchange his inept body for the quickness of bat and fleetness of foot that could carry the Senators past the hated Yankees. At least some things don't change.

Anyway, as he slips from his house in the middle of a drought-parched Washington night, his neighbor, Mrs. Something-Or-The-Other, is watering her yard in defiance of restrictions. So drought isn't a new phenomenon. Neither is selling your soul for something that seems glorious at the time.

It also points out that with all the scientific knowledge we've gained today, drought has been around in this century as long as the Yankees have. Perhaps drought isn't the most horrible thing that can happen over the course of a summer.

I'd like to put rain back in your hands. We can know everything there is to know about why it does or doesn't rain, but I don't think that brings us any closer to actually being able to regulate what falls where.

By the way, I very much appreciated the shower that blew over this afternoon. The front went through this morning and left 75 drops of rain at our house. I thought we'd gotten our weekly ration and come up short, until this afternoon, when a shower came from nowhere, with blue skies north, south, and east, and dropped ten minutes of heavy wind-driven downpour on us. Thank you. My yard appreciated the soaking and my spirit appreciated standing on the front porch watching water fall from what we still think of as heaven. We further appreciated the huge, full rainbow that followed the storm.

Was that your response to the start of this letter last night? If that was a direct response from you, perhaps I should stop writing and just be thankful. But I hope you'll remember I did tell you "thank you" as I watched the rain fall. It was a fine shower, but it wasn't enough to catch us back up. Yes, I realize it was better than no shower at all. I'm sure, as we were told when we didn't clean our plates as children, that somebody would have been happy to have what we had.

Maybe your shower this afternoon should be enough to let me know not to worry about the amount of rain. Jesus reminded us not to worry, not that his admonition stops most of us. And in the spirit of being concerned about something I can't control, and sensing an opportunity for you to get some fine press, here's what I think you should do.

The Weather Channel is always looking for a way to make 24 hours of continuous weather seem interesting, which it generally isn't unless there's a great storm out there to talk about. Perhaps they should call it the Disaster Channel instead, and just show clips of hurricanes, tornadoes, and blizzards when there's no current weather disaster in the offing. The problem with this format might be that seen enough, even a clip of an F5 tornado isn't going to continually hold someone's interest between storms.

So, in the interest of keeping the Weather Channel folk from further diversifying into all the things they might be diversifying into, such as the Locust Report, the Pagan Weather Rituals special, and the Fry an Egg on the Sidewalk Town of the Day, you might become the sponsor for the Drought Report, which already exists, but doesn't have the panache it could have with your name connected to it.

Think about it. Sam Storm comes on and says, "And now it's time for the Drought Report. The Drought Report is brought to you today by God, the Ultimate Authority on Water." Sam goes on to report on drought areas in the country with all the daunting reds and yellows signifying the depth of rain deprivation being experienced across the map.

He finishes with, "And now a word from our sponsor, God." Your message plays:

(*Black screen with sound of water dripping, steadily increasing in tempo for ten seconds until it becomes a downpour*)
Voice over: *Water....two molecules of hydrogen, one molecule of oxygen. Man...shaped from clay by my hands...Clay without water...turns to dust...Without me....so does man...Turn to me for all your water needs.*

It might work. It's simple, but effective. At least it would make people stop and think, which is a hard thing to do these days. If we all stopped and thought about you and your role as "The Ultimate Authority on Water," would you send more rain?

Oh, one other thing; I'll be on vacation starting next Thursday for five days at the beach. Take your time getting the commercial produced.

Dear God:
When you created the oceans,
were condos part of the plan?

When you gazed out over the waters of earth as they took form, as you watched the waves crash on to land never seen by human eyes, did you imagine a day when we'd swarm over the shores of the ocean, seeking to refresh our bodies and our spirits, while locked behind concrete walls and sliding glass doors? I envy the view you had in those days. At the same time, those must have been lonely days; the splendor of the seas and no one to share this most magnificent realm of creation.

I forget from yearly vacation to yearly vacation the magnificence of the ocean. I forget about the tranquil mornings and the lazy waves rolling in. I forget about the chop produced by sun-driven winds in the afternoon. I forget the sensation of a wave breaking around my body as it rushes to shore.

Each time I return, I remember, and I fall in love with the nightly sound of waves crashing and the persistent cooling breeze and the lack of responsibility away from ringing phones and job responsibilities and chores around the house. Apparently, I'm not the only one.

I can't seem to forget how many of us are out there. People, that is. All of us go away to get away and when we reach our getaway, we're in the midst of the thing we're trying to avoid. When I face away from the ocean, there are structures as far as the eye can see, look-alike structures of the mid-rise variety.

Oh, there are architectural variations in each complex, but the variations don't add any beauty to the setting. They just serve as distinguishing landmarks when I'm looking for my week's place of residence.

As a child, most our family vacations occurred at Daytona Beach, a long ride through South Georgia and down the East Coast of Florida through Jacksonville and St. Augustine. From St. Augustine to Daytona, only a smattering of houses dotted the coast. My parents once stopped to get a prospectus on a new development coming out of the ground in that stretch. Over thirty years ago, the steady march of development was underway. I suppose it's been underway since the last century in Florida, but that was the first sign for me.

In those days, I thought beaches, which is another name for a vacation resort, were in a select location and that all the area in between was just on the way. It never occurred to me we'd take it all.

As I've grown older and learned about the value of real estate as it relates to the amount of desired real estate available, I've begun to understand how things gain value. Over the last five years in particular, I've watched the pace accelerate as the economy prospered and the amount of developable beachfront property shrank.

Now, we've finally done it. We've covered the beach with condos.

You know I don't own a piece of that pie, and perhaps that's where my sadness lies. Yes, I'd love to have some beachfront property, but there's a conflicting emotion in knowing that we've taken all of it that's takeable and put something on it.

When you planned the earth, were condos part of the equation? Did you see a time when there would be massive structures towering over the edges of the magnificent ocean? Is that the price we've paid for growing up?

I've wished lately that I had lived fifty years ago when the horizons were broader and the view less obstructed. I've thought of what life would be like were it simpler and less-filled with the complications of oceanfront condos and mountaintop developments and lakes lined with houses. But in those days, like most people, I probably wouldn't have possessed the resources or the leisure time to spend at the beach.

To be more specific, God, what I actually want is an age of innocence. The one of childhood is long gone, but I want the adult version, the Adam and Eve version of walking in a garden of perfection. Sadly, I don't think I want to share it, because when there's more than one gathered together, there's a need for a condo.

We come here and gather as strangers, sharing a space of beach, sharing a pool, standing in line at restaurants. Strangers, who for the most part, want to remain that way. After a few days of seeing the same people parked on the same spot at the beach we may say hello. If our children are playing together in the sand, we might strike-up a conversation. "Where are you from?" If they're from somewhere familiar to us, we might ask if they know so-and-so, or if that certain restaurant or landmark is still there. And then we part to our own worlds, ten feet apart.

I'd ask how you keep up with all of us, but there are still more stars in the sky than people, so I suppose it isn't a big deal for you. But don't you look at your magnificent creation called earth and wonder if this jewel you've given us can accommodate the growing numbers? We seem to be stepping over each other at home and on vacation. And that may be the smallest part of the problem.

For the past couple of years as we've headed to the beach, there's been the threat of a swimming alert posed by bacteria in the water. The bacteria in the water comes from the runoff of heavy storms through that thoroughly modern invention called a storm sewer system with its pipes and retention ponds. Isn't it ironic that we've now reached a point where we're starved for rain, yet copious amounts of it pose the threat of dumping all manner of organic waste into the wellspring of life we call the ocean?

We can't find the balance between too much and too little of anything it seems. But, if I understand you correctly, part of your role as the Creator and the everyday Lord and Master of the Realm, is to bring balance into our lives. That balancing act began when you sat nature in motion and gave man dominion over the earth.

Might you help us understand the balance that's required to keep this jewel of yours in fine form and to learn to live with all of your people in dignity and grace? I know you can. I hope you will.

Let's meet again at the beach next year. It's still worth the trip.

Dear God:
Is it true there are no atheists in foxholes?

It's been said by many, though I don't know the originator, that there are "no atheists in foxholes." Only you would know whether that's true or not. I suspect there's a bit of hyperbole in that statement, but also a large measure of truth. I'm sure there are many who denied you, or at least ignored you, until those critical moments arrived. But I'm willing to bet that dyed-in-the-wool atheists probably had as hard a time seeing you in the hell of a foxhole as they did in the more pleasant aspects of creation. Maybe I'm wrong.

I've known some people who claimed to be atheists but I've never spent any time with them in a foxhole. I've spent time with them at work, and they act about the same as most of the "believing" faction, except that when they use your name in vain, I assume they don't mean it. Fact is, I've never spent time with anyone in a foxhole. If it's all the same to you, I'd rather just ask than experience the real thing.

Atheists appear to be something born out of this modern age in which we live, as are foxholes. Even in the times of the Bible, non-believers in you as The God had local gods and traditions of the supernatural. It wasn't until this century that large numbers of people began believing in nothing, so to speak. It appears there weren't many atheists until there were foxholes for atheists to be trapped in.

One of the things I'd like to know is how you view an atheist versus people who claim belief in you but don't reflect that belief in the way they live. Is there much difference between someone who professes belief in you but doesn't do much about it, and someone who professes no belief in you until he gets in a really big pinch?

I have difficulty with that question because it raises many different issues about how we perceive your daily influence on our lives.

The large measure of truth is that we seem to be able to feel you, receive your signals, or tune in to you in times of greatest crisis. No doubt it's because we're looking harder. Certainly you want us to look for you during those times, but I suspect you'd do us a lot more good if we were in touch during the rest of the times when there wasn't a crisis at hand. We might just be better equipped to deal with the crises when they come.

But sometimes I have trouble getting through, and I have to wonder if it's a matter of faith, or a lack thereof, on my part, or if I'm just supposed to "fake it till I make it" as we colloquially say.

Maybe it's the old debate of faith versus works, or as we say in more modern language, "talking the talk versus walking the walk". It crops up in the Bible and it crops up every day around us. There are those who think that believing, or expressing belief, is plenty. Some of these folks think that expressing their faith, whether anyone wants to hear it or not, is the strongest suggestion of true belief.

There are others, as James states in the New Testament, who think, "faith without works" isn't much faith at all. The idea here, as you know, is that if we have the type of relationship with you that's genuine, we'll be moved to do things as a pure reflection of your influence on our lives.

Over the centuries there have been plenty of people who practiced the idea that if they could do enough good works, they'd earn your favor. The only problem is that doing good works for the sake of doing good works is like sowing grass seed when there's no water around to make the seed grow. There's plenty of seed on the ground. The seed sower can take credit for putting it there, but without a supply of water, there's not much chance of making it grow.

Atheists, at least the nice ones, tend to believe that the growth of the human spirit is enough to make good acts a moral certainty that doesn't depend on your existence. To a degree, they're right. There are plenty of do-gooders who don't believe in you. They're out teaching people to read and they're working in soup kitchens and doing all manner of things that people who claim you exist ought to be doing. Some are doing more than those who claim you.

I'm sorry if I've rambled, but here's my point. Talking about "no atheists in a foxhole" isn't much different to me than talking about a church full of spiritually dead people who suddenly have a big crisis on their hands. When you get down to it, we're talking the same thing.

I've probably just committed some grievous theological error here, such as disregarding that not believing in you is a mortal sin, but I also recall that the Bible makes some reference to being neither hot nor cold, but lukewarm, and getting spat out as a result.

What is so difficult for me isn't having to consider whether I fit in with the hot, cold, or lukewarm crowd. I've been part of at least two. What makes me keep searching is wondering how it would be if I knew you with the certainty that an atheist who's never been near a foxhole doesn't know you.

Dear God:
Have you ever thought about giving performance appraisals?

Yes, this was the week; the week for performance appraisals. You remember last year, and you remember my reaction. This year was much better, but I can't figure out how much of this year's outcome had to do with my response to last year's appraisal. You know what they say about the squeaky wheel getting the grease.

Performance appraisals are so very human. We "appraise" each other once a year, which means the majority of feedback used in the appraisal had more to do with what someone did, or didn't do, over the past two months than over the entire year. Another old expression comes to mind. "What have you done for me lately?"

Or in the case of performance appraisals, "What have you done for me since March?" For the astute among us, March is a good time to turn up the self-aggrandizing part of our daily performance, because it's the short-term acts people remember when asked for feedback.

You'll remember that last year's appraisal was as close as I've come to walking out on a job in a long time without any reason other than proving that I didn't have to be there. You'll further remember that I didn't salvage my pride by quitting because my pride wasn't going to pay the mortgage.

Performance appraisals are at least a measurable means of understanding where your boss and your peers think you stand in terms of contributing to the old bottom line. The feedback, as my appraisal amply demonstrated in the prior year, isn't always pretty, but it sometimes provides a basis for knowing whether you're considered an asset or will soon be receiving invitations to join the company's alumni association:

Dear Mr. Baker:

Sorry things didn't work out. But you're now among friends. We're outcasts just like you. And we have a variety of reasons to hate Alpha Consolidated, most even more deeply seated than yours.

Joining our organization provides numerous benefits that even a loser like you can appreciate. Our monthly meetings feature interesting topics such as "The Rumor Mill", a half-hour discussion on all the nasty goings on at ACI. We also hold "Confession Time", a therapeutic session where alumni association members give-it-up on topics ranging from gleefully recalling office supplies they pilfered from our former mother ship to the shame that came from sucking up to someone who later turned on them.

Our organization includes focus groups for the special interests of our members: the Early Retirement group, the Dismissed for Incompetence group, the Hated My Supervisor Openly group, and many others. You can pick the one that's right for you.......

So, as you can see, there is some pressure related to performance appraisals, though the pressure shouldn't be severe unless you work for Attila the Vice President or if you've done something so unexplainably stupid there's no possible excuse that could come close to excusing you. Everyone knows it's generally a formality to go through in order to get a raise.

The imperfection of performance appraisals is regularly noted by almost everyone because the idea of changing the process comes up as often as performance appraisals; in other words, yearly. And sometimes it is changed, only to become the subject of criticism after one time through the pipeline.

Like many others, I've wondered if there is a better way. There probably is, but humans being human, it's not likely that performance appraisals will ever improve performance as much as the offer of a big bonus or the threat of dismissal.

For example, performance appraisals always include goals for the year ahead, at least in my experience. And you know as well as me that goals are statements of intention, sort of like the disclaimer that goes on an advertisement for a financial product: "Past performance is no indication of future results."

Goals sound great and I suppose would meet their lofty intent were it not for the fact that a year generally passes before anyone takes a look at the goal, hence the two-month scramble before review time. And, it's not unusual that the appraiser, reviewing the material for the first time since the appraisal, realizes that the subject hasn't been broached in nearly a year and that holding someone to a task that had a year's grace is very difficult.

I've been part of organizations that had quarterly reviews to keep things current. That's a better idea. The only problem with the quarterly reviews is that we tend to find from quarter to quarter that someone hasn't gotten around to completing a project, along with lots of valid-sounding reasons why it hasn't happened. Before you know it, another year has come and gone.

In the grand organizational scheme of things, whether an appraisal is a motivating force or not doesn't have a great impact on the overall success of the business. People are influenced more by how they are managed daily than by yearly threat or reward.

God, that doesn't mean performance appraisals wouldn't work for you. I wonder if you shouldn't think about the whole process as it applies to people. It could be safely stated that while you don't do performance appraisals in the conventional sense, you must perform some evaluation as to the progress we've made and the direction we're heading. It would helpful if we had a formal setting for getting some feedback.

While I've often resented the lack of informed effort that

went into the appraisals I've received at work, I'd like to think I'd trust you to conduct a fair hearing on my performance and offer me some direction for the coming year.

Of course, one of the things I'd have to confess up front is that I generally know whether my job performance is good or needs improving before I sit down for the appraisal. I think I'd have an even better feel about my performance in some of your categories.

I suppose one of the reasons behind performance appraisals is to reach a common understanding between two parties. For that reason only, they might be worthwhile.

If I could convince you to provide a performance appraisal for me, would you do it? What if I suggested some categories and you just provided a Likart scale type rating? For example:

· **love**
one cold individual   loves unconditionally

· **joy**
would make an onion cry   brings light to
                                                               other lives

· **peace**
loves to stir things up   calm in a storm

· **longsuffering**
skin you can see through   the patience of Job

· **gentleness**
loves to pound on the weak   sees the best in the
                                                               worst people

· **goodness**
no stranger to nastiness   can't help but do the
                                                               right thing

· **faith**
spineless   lives for the hope of
                                                               things unseen

You're right. I know how I stack up on all of these. But

somehow, if you provided a rating, I'd feel more purposeful about moving from the left of the column to the right. We could write an action plan, set some dates for making improvements, and I'd be all set.

I'd be all set until the first check-up. Then I'd have to explain why I hadn't completed some of the action items. Like everyone else, in the daily, competitive struggle to get and keep what's rightfully mine, I forget that your criteria and the criteria by which other people judge us aren't necessarily one and the same.

Or perhaps the answer has more to do with keeping a line of communication going. I haven't been getting enough daily feedback from you to have the sort of compass it takes to move in the right direction. And like a good manager, if we could stay in touch more day-to-day, perhaps an appraisal wouldn't matter at the end of the year.

Let's keep in touch.

Dear God:
Can we do away with the lines on the road?

You know the twisting road that leads to the entrance to my street. You've seen all the accidents that happened as someone tried unsuccessfully to negotiate that one nasty curve. You've heard the metal crumpling and the swearing. You've seen the tow trucks pull cars out of the ditch or up the embankment.

I just wanted to remind you of these facts because there are double yellow lines running down the middle of that road. I thought the idea was to keep the car on one side of those lines. I'm starting to see that the lines are actually suggestions instead of iron-clad laws. I guess the people who cross the lines to reach the ditch just didn't find that particular suggestion of much use.

I've also noticed that when I'm driving on that same road, I regularly meet people driving on my side of those lines. They swerve back when they see me coming, but those darn lines cause my heart to race just a bit. I begin to get concerned that since the oncoming driver is on my side of the line, there's a chance I might be involved in a collision. I know that's a silly thought. No one has hit me yet, but with those lines there I'm forced to consider the possibility.

Wouldn't we be better off if we just removed the lines? Accidents are going to happen whether the lines are there or not, so why add confusion by continuing to waste paint on these relics of a slower time. Without the lines, I wouldn't have to worry about where anyone else happened to be on the road. This move would be a great way to reduce the stress of driving. It would allow people to do all of the things they're doing in cars these days: cell-phoning, shaving, reading the paper and such, without having to worry about whether their vehicle was crossing the lines.

Don't you think getting rid of the lines is a fine idea? I'm sure that when people pray, they don't often confess to you having crossed the dividing line on the road, or for that matter, thank you for putting them there. I'm thinking no one's troubled about it, so why bother having lines in the first place?

In this same vein, could we do away with yielding right-of-way to emergency vehicles? Very few people pull over to give them a free lane anymore, so why bother with this long-held custom? With no more lines on the road, anyone can take any route they want, which should open up a lot more space for everyone. The emergency vehicles already have that same discretion. Since they're bigger than most of the other vehicles on the road, they have a much greater advantage anyway. I think it's fair.

And then there's the speed limit. I suppose it's a nice suggestion, but why force people to reduce their speed from 80 to 65 just because there's a construction zone, not that either of those speeds is below the posted speed limit anyway, but that's beside the point. Crash barricades exist for the unfortunate driver who can't navigate correctly through the maze. Why should everyone else be penalized?

Getting around in a car is difficult enough without having to deal with a bunch of impediments thrown up by legislatures and law-enforcement agencies.

There's another side to the story. We don't like boundaries because they restrict us. When we were a more compliant society, we used to think twice about running red lights and passing illegally, but we've come to understand that the odds are better of getting away with this behavior than of getting caught. And when we base our behavior on whether we get caught or not, we're setting the stage for worsening behavior and for eventual tragedy.

We're caught between the freedom of pushing the limits and the understanding that limits exist for a purpose. In the book of Galatians, Paul mentions freedom from the law, balanced by the ultimate rule of thumb: acting in a way that proves our genuine love for others. I suppose in this case, love certainly encompasses basic respect.

I wonder why we have more trouble keeping our driving and our lives between the lines these days. It seems to me that two parts of the answer have to do with speed. One is the speed of communication and the other is the speed at which we live in general. The speed of communication has made us impatient. The pace of life caused by this impatience has made us careless.

Some people on the road are completely and totally unfit to drive, but they don't account for all the bad driving, or even most of it, much the same as all societal ills don't circle back to the criminal element. Driving-wise, I think problems arise from people who are so consumed with trying to do so many things that they just aren't paying attention. Most of us are so far behind in just trying to keep up that every turn behind the wheel becomes a race.

My life off the road, as you know, is the same way. Last night, as has become our very bad habit, we were late getting in bed once again. This morning everyone slept late and we started the day off behind once more. It's now 9:31 and I should be slowing down for the night but my mind has hit high gear because in writing this I've begun to think of the frustrations of life and what I should be doing to resolve them. My child is watching television or playing a video game and my wife is somewhere in the middle thinking about what she should be doing but just doesn't have the energy to do.

I suspect there are a lot of people like us right now. People who can't slow down. I'm sure you see it every day. We're all pushing to get somewhere but none of us are quite sure where somewhere is. But if we keep pushing, we might find it. Or, we might just drive off into oblivion.

Do we want too much? Is that the problem? Are we too consumed with accumulating things? Or is it the opportunity to be part of one more self-help program or educational opportunity or one more spectacular event that is moving us at a progressively higher rate of speed?

In all this rushing around, you get lost in the shuffle. It's no wonder. Finding you takes some quiet and some contemplation. Finding you takes some time on the deck after sundown, with no noise around but the tree frogs in search of each other.

Finding you also takes some serious intent. I've noticed that you'll let me run around doing whatever I'm doing, as fast and as long as I can do it, without uttering a whisper. And I only sense you, stop to think about you, when there's enough dead air for me to consider your presence. Writing these letters has made me consider you from the perspective of who you are and what you do and how you view us. But it hasn't made my mind be quiet long enough to feel the holiness of you seep into my bones.

For you see, I realized something about you today that I've known but disregarded as out of synch with my world. What makes you different from everything else is your holiness. That's it. When my mind is quiet and open to you I find holiness, the peace of a pure spirit that transcends life as I live it. And in those moments, all things seem possible.

I know you represent healing and judgment and forgiveness and a host of other things to a variety of other people. But to me, you represent holiness, or to say it another way, the purity that makes living life without despair possible.

Ironically, some of the times I have felt your holiness most profoundly have been on long drives on uncrowded highways. Not the roads of near chaos and too-often tragedy, but those lonely stretches where driving is relaxed enough to link to thoughts of a higher calling. Maybe that's what all of us need today; a road to call our own where the only other presence is yours.

I've noticed, and so have the local and state law-enforcement authorities, that driving-related fatalities increase dramatically on the days preceding and on the Fourth of July. Drunk drivers have a lot to do with the number rising, but so do the number of cars on the road headed to unfamiliar places.

As we were driving to the lake for our annual family Fourth of July gathering, I noticed more state troopers treating people to their brand of hospitality than ever before. And for the first time in my life, I was glad to see them out in force. You know how many times I've scanned the road ahead looking for their presence, and not hopefully I might add. Maybe it's a sign of getting older, and hopefully wiser, or maybe I've seen too much on the road and in the news. I also noticed the average speed of traffic was down a good ten miles per hour. It's probably just a coincidence.

Perhaps you'll help us learn that some boundaries are created out of respect for the rest of your creation and for our own protection as well. And perhaps you'll also help us learn that there are other boundaries that keep us from finding you and your holiness that need to be crossed as often as possible.

Could we start by slowing down my engines for the night so that I can begin to appreciate the spectacular calm your presence brings?

Dear God:
What does it mean when an Asian says "Hi?"

I was leaving the grocery store a couple of days ago. On the way out, I crossed paths with an Asian fellow. I think he was Japanese. He was going in, I was going out. As our eyes met, I said, "Hi." He said, "Hi" back. What did he mean by that? Was he speaking English, or was that some defamatory comment that sounds like "Hi" in English? The Japanese have a word that sounds like "Hi" but isn't.

You're linguistically qualified to handle this question. And since it seems I'm going to be faced with all manner of foreigners here on English-speaking soil, I need a heads-up on who's messing with me when I make a simple attempt to be friendly.

I have to say up-front that this gentlemen didn't appear to be unfriendly. But he didn't show any teeth when he smiled. It was more of a tight-lipped grin, or maybe it was a grimace, or even a scowl. He had that inscrutable Asian look that leaves you wondering.

I didn't feel threatened. I was a lot bigger than him and it was broad daylight ten feet from the store's entrance, so I suppose I didn't have anything to worry about. But with people you don't know, you never know.

There are a lot of people who look like him around these days. I'm not talking about Asian males. I'm talking about people who don't look like me, or if you can get them to say more than "hi", don't sound like me. I'm not the only person who has noticed. More than a few people are starting to ask where all these people came from, and what they're doing here.

Let's get back to this fellow I met outside the door. Would Publix have anything he'd want to eat? They do have raw fish in there, but I don't think it's the kind that's eaten raw, except in the case of extreme hunger and no cooking surfaces around. And yes, they have some Chun King products, but a real live native like him wouldn't want any of that Americanized stuff; sort of like the food that's found in a Mexican restaurant, which is actually Tex-Mex, but nobody wants Tex-Mex unless it's from Mexicans, hence Mexican restaurants serving Tex-Mex food.

Which brings me to another question. Do you think the Mexicans running these restaurants are always smiling so much because we're buying food they don't eat at home?

I know I'm way off track here, but that fellow I passed in front of the store isn't part of my culture. He's not an American. He might be a Southerner, but he's not from the South of America, or South America for that matter. He's as different from me as night and day. I know he's one of your children, but wouldn't you agree all children aren't alike and able to get along?

Wouldn't he be happier with his own people? A nice little bamboo house with a carp pond in the back instead of a two-story colonial with a picket fence?

Oh, the economic angle? Well, yes it's true that we need more laborers. Thank goodness for Mexicans who think $6.00 an hour is a decent wage. And it's true we need more computer types and more engineers, so I suppose we should be thankful for Indians and Asians. And I suppose it's true that we need a little more efficiency, which would explain why we keep asking the Germans to invest money here and then move here to make sure their money is well spent. And we need some French to remind us that we're cultural pigs.

The change in the cultural landscape has been great for creating more restaurants. Black-eyed peas and collards don't hold much intrigue when you can order something from a menu that you can't pronounce from a server who can't pronounce your name.

But what happens if all of this gets out of control? What happens when the economy takes a nose-dive and the folks from overseas are laying all of us off, and we don't have any tax revenue because we gave it all away in the form of tax breaks to foreign investors to move here. What happens when the labor we've imported suddenly becomes our responsibility? Folks like me will be paying to keep all of that labor in food and housing. That can't be good for their pride or anyone's pocketbook.

Can we send them back then? I doubt it. This is a big country. It's not too awfully hard to get in or get lost.

There's another angle to this as well: mail order brides. There are men out there who can't find an American woman, or who don't like American women, or find something romantic in hooking up with someone who speaks minimal English and is grateful for the opportunity just to be here, whether she likes her husband or not. Isn't there something wrong with that? Doesn't it disappoint you that people will join themselves in holy matrimony just to get into the country? What does that say about what they'll bring to the moral climate here?

There is one further problem that will hold great interest for you. Where are these people going to find a church? They don't speak the language and if they do, they won't be familiar with the hymns. They probably don't know how to dress right for a church service on top of everything else. We are in very deep yogurt.

Of course if they don't go to church, like all real Americans do, they'll engage in all sorts of rowdy and bestial behavior. Your great land is being defiled.

Well, yes, I understand that my ancestors didn't exactly spring from the ground here, but I have proof that they were here, at least some of them, before the Revolution. And I'm sure those folks switched from French to English quickly enough; after all, they were Europeans.

It's a known fact that one of my great-grandmothers was part-Cherokee. So if anyone has a right to be here it's me. Isn't it?

Wait a minute. What does eating pork have to do with anything? All of these people we're talking about eat pork, some in very creative ways. Well, yes I remember the dream Peter had in the Bible about eating things considered unclean for a devout Jew. I remember that it became clear to him that the message of Jesus was for all people, not just your chosen. I remember all that. It's been drilled in pretty well, thank you.

But that was long ago and times have changed. Back then, no one had circled the earth. No one could hop a plane from one continent to the other. When someone needed labor, they just captured another country and made slaves of the captured. That kind of behavior isn't considered civilized today.

When you gave the people of Israel the Promised Land, you told them to clear out everyone else. They didn't and look at all the things that happened from that lack of obedience. Isn't this the new Promised Land? Aren't we the elect? We're the only Superpower left. Compassion's a fine thing, but there's a limit to what we're required to feel when the numbers keep growing. We're in charge of opportunity and there's only so much to go around.

Yes, Jesus took shortcuts through Samaria. And yes, he talked to a woman of bad reputation with no one else around. She recognized him for who he was when he couldn't get credit in his hometown. I know if you hadn't given Peter the dream about your Kingdom not being restricted, I'd be worshipping a lichen or a sea slug today.

But does any of that explain how I'm supposed to accommodate this Japanese fellow I passed the other day?

He was from Los Angeles?

Dear God: How did Jesus look on a really bad day?

I use the past tense here, because from a physical sense, it has been quite a while since he graced the earth. Nonetheless, I think I saw Jesus the other day and he wasn't looking too good. In fact, he looked more than a bit bedraggled. And since I can't say that I've ever seen Jesus before, I was wondering how he might have looked on a really bad day.

Of course, this whole proposition leads to the question that if he isn't here in the physical sense, how did I see him the other day. But see him I did.

Let's get back to the original question. I suppose from a purely physical and emotional standpoint, the worst Jesus looked had to have been on the day of his crucifixion. I think it would be difficult to argue that point.

But, there were a lot of days in 33 years, aside from that one, when things didn't go well, when physical fatigue took over and the pressure of being one of a kind set in and he looked a little worn. I think the Bible corroborates that Jesus needed to get away from it all on occasion. It would be logical to assume that physical and mental fatigue were part of the equation.

The Bible further states that Jesus gave quite a bit of himself to others, literally, in healing with the power that flowed through his earthly body, and I would think that after a while that would become a bit draining even to your son. Let's face it. He came in the human package which includes flesh and bones and muscle and particularly nerves and at some point being the center of attention becomes a drain on the structures we walk around in. Didn't he have some days when things didn't go to suit his human side?

I also recollect that the shortest verse in the Bible says, "Jesus wept." Tears are a sign of grief, which was the case then, but also a sign of fatigue or frustration or even anger. So once again I'm assuming that there were days when his human body looked at the task around him and felt like collapsing on itself.

Added to this burden was the responsibility for twelve men and a cadre of other followers who hung on everything he did, every word he said, every action he took, every expression on his face. You'd know that better than I.

As the center of all this attention, I can imagine there were days when he wanted some time alone, days when he wanted to have long talks with a trusted associate, days when making the walk to the next town seemed unbearable even to someone used to making the long walk to the next town.

Weren't there times outside the cross when he just looked frazzled and beaten down by the crush of humanity?

I just wondered because when I finally saw him the other day, he held that complex look of being completely beaten down by the world without having lost the love that drove him forward.

I stopped at a convenience store. I parked on the side of the building, where the water hose and the air pump are located. There was a man there. He had rusty blondish hair and a sun-baked complexion. When I pulled up, he was drinking from the water hose. It was hot, very hot. I was going inside for a drink after working-out in an air conditioned building. He was drinking from a hose in front of my truck. I made it past him on the way in, but only just.

When I came back out, it was just him and me on the side of

the building. He said, "Excuse me, could you spare a little change?" I'd gone in with just a couple of dollars and come back out with change in my hand.

To avoid saying no, and because his request had been reasonable, I said, as I opened the door to my truck, "How much do you need?", knowing, and thankful, I didn't have much. "If you have a dollar, that would help," he replied.

"You can have the change I have left over." As I opened my hand to see how much I had, I noted the amount. "I'm afraid I don't have but about 65 cents."

He came forward to the door of the truck for the transaction to occur. I handed him the money, thinking he'd retreat to the place on the curb beside the hose. He stood in his place instead. As I pulled the door to the truck closed, he said, "Thank you for giving me what you had. That'll help." He smiled and looked me dead in the eye and I noticed the sparkle of the same blue as mine coming from within that weathered, beaten-down face. I don't think I said anything else.

I was immediately struck by the similarity in human terms between the two of us, and I thought as I drove away, "That could be me, but it isn't." And I wondered if Jesus had that man in mind when he said, "When you've done this to the least of my brethren, you've done it to me."

As I've reflected since that time, I've thought about the humility and I've thought about the gratitude for such an insignificant gift, and I've thought about those eyes, and how close they looked to mine, and I've wondered if I were in his place if I could smile and look someone in the eye and bless them for giving so little.

And I thought that there is a timelessness to humanity that reached out from the worn face that could have been a face from 20 or 2,000 years ago.

I also thought about the countless people who have asked me

for money over the years. Maybe he was just the best at it, or maybe he was something else entirely. He didn't have that hint of desperation I've seen so many times. He didn't ask with his head ducked or his eyes darting around. He looked me straight in the eye and asked. And I responded to someone out of reflex and then realized he'd hit close to home.

I've also thought about how he came to be standing there and wondered if he wanted the money to buy a dollar's worth of beer, or even a bottle of rubbing alcohol. And frankly God, I thought, "If he can only get a dollar's worth of beer at this point in time, what does it matter if that's all he's after? What would I be after if I was him?" That's what I thought and you know it's true.

I thought that I should have offered to get him something from the McDonald's across the street. But I didn't, and my rationale, right or wrong, was that he didn't ask for something from McDonald's. He asked if I could spare a dollar. Am I supposed to decide if someone actually needs a dollar? Have you put me in charge of making that choice? Or did I not offer because giving him the change in my pocket ended my involvement for a very small price?

I don't know the answer to the broader question of giving money in those situations, but I think in this case, he was there to teach me something about giving. I think he was there to give me a lesson in looking past the obvious to see the light that burns somewhere down in all of our souls. I'm glad I gave him the change. I wish I'd done it in a different spirit.

And there's something else I didn't think about until later. He was there because he didn't have anywhere else to be. Yet, he could look me in the eye and smile with the innocence I could never summon in that situation.

He didn't look very good at all, but his gaze looked a lot better than most I'd seen that day. Was that how Jesus looked on his worst day? Did his body look beaten while his eyes were at peace?

Dear God:
Should I stay away from old cars?

Or should I just stay away from selling them? Is it possible that whenever one of my clunkers has become expendable, the best course of action is to give it to a charity? I'd get the satisfaction of helping someone else and get a tax deduction for my generosity. I'm starting to think that the time invested in selling a 12-year-old car might not be the most productive time I'll spend.

You know what a fine car the LeSabre was over the ten years it was in our possession. It provided reasonable, safe, cost-effective transportation. The passenger, side-view mirror was in the trunk, and the power windows didn't work on either of the front windows. The fuel gauge stuck at the quarter-tank mark, and the gear indicator didn't move past reverse any more. The vacuum hose that made the cruise control function no longer created a vacuum. But, the car ran like a top.

The paint was flaking on the hood and faded to yellow on the formerly black rubber section of the bumpers, but the body remained in overall fine shape. It took us a lot of places and did so without complaining or requiring any major surgery.

Oh, I know it jerked a little between gears because the engine mounts were worn, but in relative terms the cost of replacing the mounts wasn't major. The small leak in the oil pan wasn't a big deal to take care of either.

175

So when it came time to sell it, I thought it would go quickly. I priced it to move, as the car dealers say, and I figured for $1,350, give or take what was whittled away in negotiating, someone would get a decent car to tool around in and we'd have a small rebate on a car that paid for itself many times during the years of not having a car payment.

But what I didn't know, or perhaps what I'd forgotten, was the ordeal that comes with selling a car. I figured that for $1,350 or less people would be happy to have basic transportation that ran well. I was prepared to deal on it so that we could remove its cost from our car insurance bill and because when something's no longer part of the plan, it's best to take the money you can get for it and move on.

What I wasn't prepared for were a couple of car-buying variables that I'd forgotten since my last venture into car sales. I'd forgotten that even if you're asking next to nothing for a car, the person who might spend that next to nothing wants to spend it for a reason and expects your car, in relative terms, to undergo the same scrutiny that a nearly new model undergoes. If they could afford more they'd pay more and wouldn't have to worry about whether the machine in question would run three months and die.

I had rehearsed my basic pitch, "It has a good engine, good tires, has never required a major repair, has never been wrecked and most of the paint's still there...it's a good deal for what I'm asking." I still found myself immediately feeling the need to defend the LeSabre's virtues to prospective buyers. I was a bit miffed by people who didn't want to look at the car when I said the paint was a bit faded or that the cruise didn't work. I felt put upon by people who wanted me to change my schedule for them to look at the car. I was practically giving it to them.

The other variable I'd forgotten is that every buyer of a car has a story about why they need to purchase a car in the first place. In the case of a 1988 Buick LeSabre, the buyers didn't want to purchase the car because they had a soft spot in their hearts for the cars that rolled off the assembly line in that particular year. They hadn't been scanning the classifieds for months hoping against hope that a 1988 LeSabre with 161,000 miles would be there.

They needed a car, a cheap car, because things had happened in their lives that put them in the position of needing a cheap car. And, as you know, there's something about the human condition that makes people feel the need to explain why they are actually interested in buying a relic like an '88 Buick. I guess they didn't want me to think they had wasted their lives to the point of needing something that even I didn't want anymore.

What my experience told me is that a 1988 Buick LeSabre is the car of choice for people getting a divorce. Male or female, it's the car of choice. Or perhaps anything with an asking price of $1,350 is the car of choice for recent divorcees.

The first prospect, a man, still had the other key to the Lexus to prove that not too long ago he wouldn't have come near the car. The second prospect, a woman, had my ear for a bit on what happens when the wife signs both cars over to the husband without consulting an attorney first. Perhaps what they were both after was a story that would lower the price. In both cases, I just wanted to move the car, and as the dealers also say, "No reasonable offers refused."

Maybe they just wanted to communicate to another person how they came to be at this point in their lives. Maybe part of selling a car, or selling anything for that matter, is learning to listen and understand the deeper things that are happening in people's lives that aren't necessary for the actual transaction, but very necessary for the daily transaction of relating to other people.

In any event, both people wanted the car. They made their offers. I countered with a couple of negotiating points and sold it twice. The man, my first buyer, had cash and wanted the car immediately. He didn't even test drive it, which proves that he knew a deal when he saw one. It might also prove that if you level with people in great detail about every problem that car has, at some point they believe you when you tell them that it runs well and will get you around town if that's all they need.

I even mentioned to him that the battery light had popped on that afternoon and that I'd had some problems with the battery connection, but that I'd resolve the issue before he took the car. He made his offer, which was several hundred dollars less than I wanted. But I told him I'd accept it if he'd take care of the battery, which he agreed to do.

I should have had the title and bill of sale with me. As you'll remember, I drove home to pick them up. On the way back, the car died one mile from our agreed meeting spot and I had the opportunity to do a little pushing to get it out of the road. I lost that sale since it was obvious the battery light was pointing to the alternator and not the battery.

The second buyer knew about the alternator, and all the other problems up front. We agreed on a price that included the $80 it took to get a rebuilt alternator stuck under the hood. She wanted to have her father look at the car first, since he was fronting the money for this particular investment. She told me he was a tough customer, and even though she knew it was by far the best car she'd seen, particularly for the price, he'd want to take a little something out of my hide just to be satisfied he'd cut a good deal.

So I sat on the car and waited for a time for him to be available. As you'll remember, it took a week for us to meet. I thought driving into one of the stalls of the do-it-yourself car wash as lightning popped all around us was a dramatic climax to the deal.

I don't know how much you and this guy talk, but he knows cars. He knew that by putting on the parking brake and then giving the car a little gas in drive and then reverse that it was possible to tell which motor mounts were worn. It turned out both, but I'd already been up-front about that. He knew to test the power locks on the doors to make sure each door worked. And of course you'll remember the lock on the back door of the driver's side started sticking a few years back. I think I'd told them about that.

He knew how to check the tire wells for repair work from an accident. Fortunately, that car played no part in any bad driving I've done. He knew everything. He went over that car with the practiced eye of a forty-year fraud investigator who has seen it all and forgotten nothing.

I was glad I'd been very up-front about the car. I couldn't have pulled anything over on this guy. I suppose honesty is the best policy after all. Particularly when the real buyer turns out to be the Einstein of used-car evaluation.

As it was, I didn't mind splitting the $100 difference between us to seal the deal. He got me off the price. She got a good car. I got $1,050 that I'm sure will disappear faster than oil does from that old truck I took on before sacrificing the LeSabre. But it's gone and my insurance company will have to learn to live without the premiums until we invest in something else down the road.

You know, God, selling that car was a lot of trouble. I think I know now why I'd put off doing so for three months. I knew it would be a headache, and it was. But I also learned a few things from the experience that should help me down the other roads I travel every day.

I learned that putting off something that needs to be done isn't going to make it any easier when I finally get around to doing it. In fact, it made it a lot harder, because pushing that car in April would have been a lot cooler than pushing it in July.

Maybe I could learn something about my relationship with you in that respect, too. When I have a clear sense that there's something that needs doing on your behalf, I need to get on with it, no matter the dozen rationales I can think of to make it next week or next month or next year.

I learned that until you deal with people who you wouldn't

be thrown together with otherwise, you won't be aware of what other people's lives might be like as you breeze past them every day. And I must admit to you, there's a limit to how much I want to know about someone else's life. At the same time, understanding that the world is full of people who have all sorts of things going and those sorts of things make them act in predictably bad and unpredictably good ways is a big step toward loving our neighbor as much as we love ourselves.

I also learned that when you've been driving the same car for ten years and are ready to move on because you've found something else you wanted more, you might find in getting rid of that car that you had something pretty special to serve you so well for all those years. I suppose that's true of our best relationships, our best jobs, our best dogs. We don't appreciate them after we've had them awhile until we've moved on to something else.

As I turned it over this afternoon, I felt a sense of appreciation for all the loyal service that car provided. I just hoped it wouldn't betray me by breaking down on its new owner on the way home.

Dear God:
Have you ever sat on the bench outside Wal-Mart?

I learned something else about life when I sold the car. Remember when I turned it over to its new owner in the parking lot of Wal-Mart? We filled out the information on the bill of sale, went through the rite of handing over keys, and went our own ways. She drove off in her new car and I was left to wait in the Wal-Mart parking lot until my wife picked me up.

A Wal-Mart parking lot in the middle of summer, or I suppose the rest of the year for that matter, is not a prime spot to hang out. But the bench in front of Wal-Mart, between the entrance and exit doors, is not an uninteresting location. Have you ever sat there and watched us go by? You should. Of course, you see each of us every day so maybe it wouldn't hold the same fascination for you that it did for me, but the view from that bench is a good place to gain a slice-of-life perspective.

Can I tell you what I saw? Maybe we could compare notes.

My first thought upon sitting down was to wonder what people coming and going from the store would think of me. Would they wonder why I was sitting there, and if so, what would their impression be? I've noticed people sitting on that bench before and I've wondered what *they* were doing there. Part of the wondering I've done had to do with how they looked. I don't mean how they were dressed or how their hair looked. I wondered because of the expressions their faces carried.

There have been a few that I fully expected to spring up and grab me by the throat while they muttered some unintelligible threats at me. I've expected a few to ask me for something, most likely money.

Others have looked impatient or tired or frustrated and some looked neutral. I decided neutrality was the expression to adopt so that no one would think I was about to grab them by the throat and mutter at them and feel the need to report me to one of the greeters. So I sat and looked neutral.

I suppose you don't or wouldn't worry about what people would think if you were sitting there on the bench. Whether I like to admit it or not, I am concerned about what other people think about me, but then I'm one of them and you aren't, so I suppose my insecurity in that situation is understandable.

The other part of the equation is of course the social stigma of sitting on a bench outside Wal-Mart. For some of us, there's a societal status message about where we're seen sitting around. For me, that bench at Wal-Mart could easily create the impression that I had no other place to be, which means that my value in life couldn't be very high if I was just parked there for no apparent reason.

A cure for this impression would have been to hold a small placard that announced, "Just sold my car. Waiting for my wife to pick me up." Of course, holding such a placard would have created some other impressions that might have been even less desirable than sitting there without any explanation.

What I looked or didn't look like and what I saw are two completely different things. I was asking you about the view from there because I suppose you get a similar view every day from all sorts of places and I don't, so it was a bit of a revelation to me. I noticed, as I have a lot lately, that the world's full of people.

What I noticed particularly in this case was the manner in which people approached the store. Since I was sitting in my neutral posture with my neutral expression, I became sort of invisible. I know I was invisible because almost no one paid me the slightest bit of attention. There was no furtive eye contact, no sidelong glances, nothing of the sort. And in my invisibility, I had the opportunity to watch the world up close. Maybe that's what you do all the time, too.

I watched two people who appeared to be perfect strangers walk into the store. These people, a middle-aged woman and a teenage girl/woman appeared to be related. They were reasonably close together physically, but for all intents and purposes, it appeared they might as well have been miles apart.

I watched a family walk in that consisted of two parents and two small children. They weren't speaking to each other either. But maybe the difficulty of getting two small children to stay in line requires a lot of concentration. Or perhaps both parents knew that if they kept the pace up, they might be able to enter the store without having to hear a request to ride on the small mechanical horse near the entrance. Or maybe they decided that I *didn't* look neutral and just wanted to escape inside without having to make eye contact.

What they didn't know is that both of the children made eye contact with me. Actually, they didn't make eye contact because I had on sunglasses, but they looked at me with the pure innocence with which only a child can stare at someone.

You know I'm not above making faces at children when standing in line and while their parents are looking the other way. Doing so is my litmus test for whether a child is truly cool or not. A cool child will giggle, and likely get in trouble with a parent. Uncool children will bury their heads in the closest part of the parent's anatomy, which also brings parental wrath.

Maybe I shouldn't do that, but I like children, and the only way you can communicate with them without tipping off the parent is to make faces. If you say something to the child, you then have to either talk to the parent or face the possibility that the parent thinks you're some kind of creep.

In this case, I didn't bother making a face or even smiling because doing so would have destroyed my neutrality. A middle-aged man talking to children from the bench at Wal-Mart would not have been the most savvy thing I've ever done.

My other observation, while spending my ten minutes on the bench, was the pace of everyone going in and out. I assume all of these people like Wal-Mart because they were all in a hurry to get in, but I noticed the people coming out the other side were in an equal hurry to leave. Well, yes, the parking lot temperature was probably 150 degrees at the time, but I don't think that explains all of it.

For those exiting, it might have been that standing in a line that stretched back to sporting goods in order to purchase shampoo and some 20-pound test line might have put them in the mood to move on. For those entering, hurrying in might have been an attempt to beat the person going in the store in front of them to their place in line.

I don't know the answers. I don't suppose it really matters. I bring this up only because no one was hanging around outside the store. There weren't a bunch of old guys comparing hardware purchases. There weren't any women talking about what was going on down at the beauty shop. There were just people, moving on. And there I was parked on the bench and completely anonymous.

Maybe you could project your voice into the store every now and then so that people would at least stop and ask each other, "What was that?" It might lead to a conversation about hardware or goings on at the beauty shop. Or it might make people wonder if the new greeter had a voice that sounded like God's.

Dear God:
When did country music start sounding like Robin Trower?

I had a flashback yesterday, and it came from a most unusual place. I tuned the radio dial to what was a country station when I last checked. From the car's speakers came a sound straight from 1976. It sounded like something from a live Robin Trower eight-track I played into warped submission that summer. Lots of synthesizer noise building to a crescendo; sort of a space music feel without the tranquillity.

I rechecked the dial and it was set where I'd thought it was when I changed to that station. But that was no country music playing. As I listened, the strident cacophony changed to a modified country twang followed by the dulcet tones of Reba McIntyre belting out "Fancy." I now know it was the intro for the start of a Reba show, but it sure didn't sound country.

It did sound like something someone would play to jack up the crowd prior to a football game or a wrestling match or, for that matter, a concert. I scratched my head a bit because I'm accustomed to recognizing music by the particular notes, rhythms and instruments that identify country, rock and so on.

You've probably noticed today that people throw around the term genre a lot, which means the same thing as I just said but sounds a lot more sophisticated. In this case, the genre I attached to the intro sounded more like something from mid-70's rock than it did Reba's stage show.

185

Though I've never seen Reba perform, I imagine there's quite a difference in how her concert spectaculars looked and sounded ten years ago as opposed to how they look and sound today. Ten years ago, I imagine the show began with someone with a great radio voice saying, "Ladies and Gentlemen, please welcome Reba McIntyre." The band hit the opening notes and the spotlight hit Reba—beginning of show.

I imagine the Robin Trower intro required a great deal of stage fog with Reba descending to the stage from the murky heights of the coliseum superstructure; mind-altering, but not very country.

These days, as I'm sure you've noticed, in a lot of literal and figurative arenas the lines are more than a little blurred. The normal distinctions we've always been able to lay on people and places and types of music don't hold anymore. The reason the lines have blurred is that someone in the country music business discovered they weren't selling country music. They were selling entertainment.

These same people understand the name *country* sometimes gets in the way of people buying CDs or attending concerts who might show up otherwise if there was no clear label on the performer (which is another way of saying musician). The other thing they've figured out is that you can call music *country* on a country station while you don't call it by anything but the song title when it gets air play somewhere else.

I don't know how much you care about what's been happening with the country music scene, but I know you're aware of the number of big stars out of Nashville who have been getting their music played on stations that would go out of the way to avoid playing country music. Of course, by the time one of these performer/musicians gets a song on the non-country stations it doesn't sound like country any more. It sounds like what we call "pop."

The hottest thing going in country music, at least in my opinion, is Faith Hill. I'm sure you like her name. How you feel about her music I wouldn't venture to guess. But to my feeble ear, she has a lot of talent. I heard her sing "The Star Spangled Banner" prior to the start of Super Bowl XXXV. She didn't sing the national anthem like someone from Mississippi who gained her initial fame singing country music. She sounded like a mainstream voice from anywhere in the United States.

She's made a quick but careful transition from a country singer to a mainstream diva, another of those ridiculous words that's found favor these days, in this case to describe any top, pop female voice. I remember the first time I heard a Faith Hill song. I didn't know it was her until recently. She was belting out a very country version of Janis Joplin's "Take a Little Piece of My Heart." No one would have accused her of anything at the time except being country.

Faith Hill is now one hot item in marketing terms. She has a big endorsement deal selling wireless phone service, a deal she'd never have gotten if she'd kept singing country versions of Janis Joplin tunes.

She's not alone. Many country performers have found that, like the Doublemint Gum commercials, you can have twice the fun with the same product if you can dress that product up to sell it to a different market.

What this rush for wider acceptance means in broader terms is the subject of my curiosity. Marketing people, within whose ranks I occasionally count myself, sometimes use the expression, "You aren't selling the steak, you're selling the sizzle." Of course, what the expression means is that what people buy isn't the product but the image the product creates.

Country singers can make a lot more money by not sounding quite so country. Specialty stores can be quite successful selling ordinary t-shirts with their name on them at big mark-ups if they've cultivated the right image.

Is all this working against your church? I've heard it said of late that most people don't find the church relevant to their daily lives any more. They're proving their perceptions by doing what consumers do. They're shopping for whatever they want or think they need somewhere else.

It raises the question of what your church should be doing to compete in this image-driven, thrill-of-the-moment world. The natural reaction might be to carefully craft our own image that crosses over into the mainstream. If country doesn't have to be country anymore, why should the church have to be, for example, about a relationship with you? But the church is different, or at least I think it is. The church has to stand for something unchanging if it is to truly be the church. It relies on timeless truths that revolve around you. And without those beliefs at the center, it's just not worth very much.

Of course, the church doesn't appear to be worth a lot to the majority of people right now. Polls show that while a lot of Americans believe in something, and in most cases that's some version of you, they don't believe in churches as the ticket for finding or keeping whatever they believe in. It might be that churches could take a cue from Reba. We'd just sing "Rock of Ages" in place of "Fancy" but dress it up with some fog and lifting devices.

A few churches out there that have done just that. They've decided that putting on a great show is a quick way to draw a crowd. If people are drawn to wrestlers that glide in on cables, or singers that appear out of the fog, why shouldn't they be given the same thrill for showing up at a worship service?

Maybe that approach is fine with you, but it doesn't sit very well with me. The difference, as best I can tell, is that a church worship service is supposed to provide something that both integrates into and transcends daily life. In fact, it's actually supposed to be about you.

I'm sure that a well-produced pop music performance has people buzzing around the break room at work the next day, but it's fleeting at best, until the next show comes to town. A church can also put on a great show that could be equally popular the next day but not really point anyone in your direction.

Maybe we're missing the point because we can't decide if you're supposed to be a great thrill or a low and steady tune we hum all the time. Or maybe what you offer is so different that we have trouble separating modern image-making with the substance you represent. If people's lives were truly being affected by their relationships with you, the type of worship service a church put on wouldn't make much difference. They'd find you in the light coming through the windows or in the squeak of a loose floorboard.

Maybe what we're missing today are lives that can be distinguished from one or a hundred others. We're so accustomed to being part of the mass market that we lose sight of the individual contributions to your world that are produced by true spiritual growth.

Perhaps we need to understand that quite a few country musicians have no pretense of being otherwise and are doing quite well though they aren't pleasing everyone, that many businesses have stuck to the idea that high-value delivery of a product is image enough, and that you have people out there who find you daily without having high-voltage charges flowing into their bodies.

Might it not be time to reassert yourself as the God who understands people need the steak of substance and not the sizzle of image? Maybe in time we'll see that a life lived with daily purpose has a refreshing uniqueness to it that stands out from the crowd without further assistance.

And when that happens, maybe churches will find the living out of your basic truth sells just fine. And just maybe, country music performances won't need synthesizers and smoke machines to be worth seeing.

Dear God:
What's so uniting about
the United Way?

I'd like to ask you to take a moment and consider something with me. Let's suppose that someone had the bright idea that by pooling all the money available to meet human needs in the community, there would be less duplication in services and more efficient use of the pool of dollars available.

And let's suppose this same person managed to pull it off. The charities, or service organizations, agreed to be part of the pool. Businesses agreed it was better to make one lump-sum donation and run one charitable appeal than to be faced with appeals year round.

Let's further suppose this approach caught fire across the country. Before you knew it, this fine idea was a national organization.

While we're at it, let's suppose someone realized the distribution of available funds is a decision best made at the local level.

Let's see. We have one big organization that covers the entire country with local organizations that raise and spend the money locally with some knocked off the top to give to the national organization for its administrative and marketing efforts.

You know, of course, that I'm talking about United Way.

You are also aware that I've run the United Way campaigns at work over the past two years and what I've learned from the experience. I've learned people can be unexpectedly generous, just as I've learned people can be unexplainably negative.

After the recent campaign, I've had to ask myself if the United Way is in fact uniting. You know the moments of anger, dismay, and, yes, gratitude I have felt during our campaign. We had a great campaign in monetary terms. I ought to be beside myself with thanks for those who gave. But I must admit, I came out of the campaign with a bittersweet taste.

I ran into a form of opposition from some that I'd seen the previous year. It was opposition born of giving to something considered secular. This year there was a specific secular target. This target didn't have anything to do with opposition to helping abused women or disadvantaged children or hungry people. It had to do with the Boy Scouts.

You'll remember that the Boy Scouts went to court to fight for their right to exclude homosexuals as troop leaders. The Scouts won when the court ruled that private organizations had the right to select who they wanted in their organization.

This ruling sat well with people who don't like homosexuals and didn't sit well with people who like homosexuals. I know I'm oversimplifying, but when you take away all of the rhetoric, that's about what the case boiled down to. The implications went much further. I found that abused women or disadvantaged children or hungry people don't stand a chance when it comes to taking a stand against homosexuals, even when there's no stand to take.

Some United Way's in places far from here decided to punish the Boy Scouts for their lack of inclusiveness by withholding United Way funding from the Scouts in their community. The United Way here had no such plans. I didn't have any idea it was an issue.

I didn't have any idea until I started getting feedback from people. These folks informed me that, since the United Way wasn't funding Boy Scouts anymore, they weren't giving to the United Way. This was news to me since I knew the Scouts were one of the top ten recipients of United Way funding in our county.

A few more historically steady donors didn't give at all which left me wondering if they voted silently in the same direction.

I responded to the people who told me they weren't giving because of the Scout issue by acknowledging their right not to give a dime. I reminded them that the Scouts were major recipients of United Way dollars in our county and that, by not giving to the United Way, they were denying the Scouts and other deserving charities needed funding. It didn't work.

What's puzzling to me about this situation is that the people who communicated directly to me about the issue are bright, sensible people whom I respect. In this case, we might as well have been talking in different languages.

Here's where I need your help.

My experience in two years of dealing with the United Way is that some people who claim you as the center of their existence don't like the United Way because they consider it secular and liberal and un-You-ly. They don't like how the money's spent, or they see this pooling of resources as some great conspiracy to foist humanism on the community.

This same group of people by and large also think the government ought to get out of the human service business. They don't want the United Way to do the job. They don't want the government to do the job. That leaves, let's see, churches or service organizations.

It has been said that, if churches were carrying out the mission Jesus gave them to carry out, we wouldn't need the United Way or charities or government intervention. If these folks don't want the government or the United Way to compensate for society's ills, it must be that their churches are taking care of all these pressing needs in society. You know better. I know better. They know better.

There's a very deep-seated issue among us. Much of the church today has taken your command to be "in the world but not of it" to places I don't think that command was intended to be taken. They've become very centered on themselves and centered on the idea that only they stand unbent in the continuing destruction of society.

Their response has been to pull away from society and keep themselves pure from all the nastiness that's part of living here every day. Their lives are spent holding each other's feet to the fire and openly, or secretly, hating everyone who disagrees with them.

I can't be sure of this, though you are, that someone started a rumor that the Scouts were being defunded here and it spread. It was one of your people, and other people listened and never questioned. Is that how you want things to run?

Do you want people, all of whom were created in your image, to take as truth what someone who carries the badge of faith says without every stopping to consider if it's truth or not? If you do, please send me in the direction of someone who is always right and has a direct, incontrovertible pipeline to you. I'll never ask another question.

Can you understand my frustration? Some of your people are the ones in this case who were all too willing to believe something that was false and then spread a rumor. I believe the Bible speaks to that issue.

Could it be that all people of faith need to realize that blackened hearts are the way for all of us? Have they forgotten the old saying, "There but for the grace of God go I?" In their rush to punish one segment of society, they seem to have forgotten that the innocent get killed in wars, cultural or real.

I don't understand. I don't understand at all, which leads me to wonder if they're right or I'm right. Is United Way so uniting after all?

Dear God:
What will become of
Floyd Padgett?

For many years, a comforting sight has been near eye-level on every elevator I've entered in South Carolina. Floyd Padgett had been there before me and officially affixed his signed approval on the trustworthiness of the elevator.

I never met Mr. Padgett, but I'd seen his form of graffiti enough to take comfort in his legal defacement of elevators throughout the state.

Several months ago, there was an article in the paper covering Mr. Padgett's retirement from Elevatordom. As I recall, Mr. Padgett planned to travel during his retirement. In a bit of newspaper feature article repartee, the writer made reference to the fact that, wherever Mr. Padgett traveled, there would be elevators to be ridden.

The story also noted that, due to the number of elevators in the state, Mr. Padgett had numerous inspectors who did the actual inspecting, but his name went on the elevator certificate of operation, giving an air of consistent authority when you experienced it statewide.

I paid even more attention to Mr. Padgett's signature for a short period after that. It became a great way to break the elevator ice. "I see Floyd Padgett beat me to this elevator again." I'd find that I wasn't the only one who had noticed his signature over the years. In fact, most people, it seems, knew his name as a matter of course. In South Carolina elevator circles, Floyd Padgett was a very famous man.

A couple of weeks ago, I noticed that Mr. Padgett's signature was no longer affixed to the certificate of operation on either elevator in our office building. The new elevator inspecting czar's name was there in neat script with a little artistic initial buried in the middle. An inspection had been held of our elevators since Mr. Padgett's retirement. What the experience told me was that we move on.

At that moment, I couldn't remember Floyd Padgett's name. As soon as the new signature was on the certificate of operation, it was as if Mr. Padgett's name had never been affixed. I asked countless people on the elevator if they could remember the "name of the guy whose signature had been there for years and just retired." Everyone knew who I was talking about, but no one could produce a name.

After a week of blank stares and no answers, I asked my wife if she could remember his name. She started out with Patterson. "Was it Floyd Patterson?" Unless former heavyweight boxing champions move into the elevator business as a second career, it wasn't likely. I also knew she was close. It took a moment, but it came to me: Floyd Padgett.

I suppose I could go to a psychologist with this question and get an answer, but you created our processing sequences. Perhaps you can help me. As soon as someone else's name appeared on the elevator certificate of operation, why were many people, including me, unable to remember his name? I don't know how long Mr. Padgett had the job, but I'm sure it was a number of years, and I was absolutely sure his name would be engraved in my memory in any elevator I rode in South Carolina.

But it wasn't. He retired, an inspector visited, and his name was replaced as part of the daily routine. Is it that we remember people who are part of our lives as long as they have familiarity and utility? Mr. Padgett certainly had familiarity unless one took the stairs instead of the elevator, and he certainly had utility in providing the assurance of safe passage to elevator riders throughout the state.

Or, did I forget because we never actually met? I've never met a living President, yet I know all their names. To my way of thinking, Mr. Padgett was more a part of my daily life than any of our country's chief executives, yet, as soon as someone else's name went up, I couldn't remember *his* name.

He's now off visiting other places and doing the things that retired people do. I hope retirement is a chance for him to put his years of work behind him, but I'm troubled that I could put his name behind me as quickly as I did. Maybe I couldn't remember his name because our association was frequent, but brief, and never in person. I'm sure that's part of my forgetfulness.

Forgetting Mr. Padgett's name made me think about people who have been part of my life in the past with whom I swore I'd never lose contact. There are people in other states, people in other towns, people just across town, and even a few just up the road; and we seem to lose touch. Of course, most of them haven't been in touch with me either, so it's mutual.

Life goes on, and people lose touch. While I've grappled with this issue before, I suppose I'm asking today for a special reason. As you know, my uncle, who had been a large part of my life for forty-two years, headed in your direction Thursday evening. You know how sick he'd been, and, while I haven't gotten used to the idea that he's no longer among us, I can say with certainty that his future now is much brighter than it was a week ago.

He reached the age of eighty-one, after working until he was in his early seventies. He was a charming, well-known person and spent most of his life with people tugging on him this way and that for one reason or the other. After he retired, I noticed there weren't as many people tugging as before. His circle shrank considerably. I know, in part, the reason his circle of acquaintances shrank had to do with his health. He was the classic case of someone who worked many years and then retired to find his body retiring at the same time.

But that doesn't explain how all the people he called friends weren't around as much anymore or around at all. I know what happened. People moved on, and he moved toward a quiet retirement. We're all driven to do what we must do to get our backs scratched in one way or the other, and he wasn't in the back-scratching business anymore. Once he retired, other people moved to fill in the very large space he'd created in the world around him.

I think he felt a bit bewildered to be in a world where relationships built around work and civic duty didn't consume his time. I felt sad watching all of this transpire because I knew how much energy he drew from being around others. I've wondered in the last few days how long he might have lived had he stayed on the move.

His funeral is in a couple of days, once everyone gets back from wherever they went for their Labor Day holiday. Like Mr. Padgett, I wonder how many people remember him, not his name, because I doubt anyone will forget they knew him. I wonder how many people will remember how much he meant to them for so long.

The interim between his death and his burial has been a time of reflection for me because I realized that the space he filled in my life for so many years shrank in each of the past few years. You know the guilt I feel over our diminished contact.

If there's any consolation in all of this, I can say that I filled his space primarily with my son. On the occasions when we did see each other, particularly in the past few months when getting out of bed was an effort for him, I could report on how my son was doing with his golf game, the same game my uncle taught me almost forty years ago.

Why is it so difficult to overpower expediency by acting on the best of intentions? Maybe there's a lesson I can learn from this experience for the rest of my days. I hope you'll help me to continue seeing the value in the lives that have touched me so well for so long.

There are two other things for which I hope: that Mr. Padgett finds that the world doesn't end at the top floor of a building and that my uncle finds that a golf ball off the screws of a three-wood travels at the speed of light in heaven.

Dear God:
Did you invent the
Pareto Principle?

You're much better acquainted with Vilfredo Pareto than I. I've become familiar with his work and the other work it inspired, and it's fascinating stuff. What I learned was that Pareto was an Italian economist who studied the distribution of wealth in the British economy and several others.

He found what you've known since man's been around. In almost any economy, 20% of the people hold 80% of the wealth. He further found that the circle of wealth grew even tighter toward the top end of wealth holders. His research showed that, in then present-day England and in economies throughout history, it was predictable that 10% of the people held 70% of the wealth and 5% of the people held up to 50% of the wealth. Pareto called this recurring fact of life a "predictable imbalance." We call it the "rich getting richer and the poor getting poorer."

From his study, we have the "Pareto Principle."

Unfortunately, Mr. Pareto never thought to question if this phenomenon might apply to anything outside economics. We now know it does. In almost all systems of human creation, the 80/20 rule, as Pareto's predictable imbalance is also known, is an accepted fact.

Taking Pareto's model, other people have done research on issues outside economics. Their research has shown, for example, that in any organization, 80% of the work is produced by 20% of the people, 80% of a company's profits come from 20% of its product or service output, 80% of the crimes are committed by 20% of the criminals, and on and on it goes.

Since you created people, my question, put another way is, "Did you put some system in place that makes the 80/20 rule apply in almost anything we do?" Is the 80/20 rule as much your doing as the orbit of our solar system around the sun, the changing of seasons, or ten digits on each set of appendages?

There's a reason for asking you this question. Do you put certain things in motion that seem to be of human construction but affect our lives in a predictable-as-the-rising-and-setting-of-the-sun way?

If, in fact, you put in place whatever determines how humans function together behaviorally as evidenced by the Pareto Principle, should I then not worry about the downstream consequences this pattern points out? Or, should I be trying to change the aspects of it that don't exactly square with my understanding of you?

There's an opposing question. "Is the Pareto Principle of human origin?" It's natural to reason that if 20% of the people produce 80% of the output, they should reap the rewards of their efforts. But there's a bigger question. What determines who those 20% of people turn out to be?

It's been my experience that people who succeed in human terms are one of three things: very aggressive, very smart, or very disciplined. Do you make us extremely aggressive or extraordinarily smart or highly disciplined, or is it learned or inherited or both?

All of these questions go to the heart of our religious systems. In our attempt to explain you, we've come up with all sorts of ideas about how you work on these very issues just mentioned. For example, there are some, and the number is growing these days, who believe that you create and call select people in your name and that everyone else is pretty much out of luck. What these folks don't say is that other people become one of the select by joining their club and espousing their tightly held views, which are correct because only they can represent you. In that sense, it's like a religious fraternity with a slightly different pledge process.

My experience with these folks is that they've resurrected this idea to feel better about themselves and the positions they've chosen. If you can throw everyone else out of the loop, there's no need to consider whether their difference in belief has any merit or not. This idea of the "select" among us is more an indication of the polarization that's occurred in our society than it is of sound thought about you. That's my opinion, and I'm not one of the select or someone would have let me know by now.

I do like to think that I'm part of your plan. I assume other people would like to know where they fit into your plan as well. Knowing if we're part of the 20% or not would be helpful.

Knowing if we're part of the 80% not producing the most might also be helpful if we had some indication that the role we play has significance. I'd like to be part of the 20% who does more and has more meaning in my life to show for it. But at least 80% of us would be just fine knowing we were doing the right things for the right reasons, whether that put us in some upper echelon or not.

Should we be worried that in human systems there are people who will come out on top? Or should we be more concerned that in our relationship with you we're focusing on the 80% of our lives that will be most productive from your standpoint?

If the Pareto Principle is your creation, the 80% you consider important doesn't appear to be the 80% on which we're focused. Jesus paid little or no attention to government, fashion, or the accumulation of wealth. He was interested in bring-

201

ing people closer to you. He didn't worry about the rest.

My son is working on his "writer's notebook" for English. I suggested he do a section on what he'd do if he had $20 million. He pointed out that at his age he couldn't have $20 million without our administering it in some way, which I guess is true. We've never been presented with that particular problem.

In this hypothetical situation, my son would be part of the inner sanctum of the Pareto Principle. He would hold a disproportionate amount of wealth, probably in the top two percent of the population. Unless he was foolish, he, his children, and his children's children's children would never run out of a steady source of upper-income wealth.

In this letter full of questions, I have to ask one more. If he's part of the top 20%, even the top 1%, is he then responsible in your eyes to look after the bottom 20%? When Mary Magdalene used expensive perfume to wash Jesus' feet, his disciples criticized the waste of money it represented and suggested it could be spent more effectively on the poor. Jesus replied with a statement that has been abused since that time. "The poor are with you always."

Pareto's findings confirmed the facts of what Jesus said: The poor *are* always with us. Pareto spent the rest of his life talking about this inequity. Jesus provided a simple, sufficient answer to the same issue. "Whenever you've done this to the least of (other people), you've done it to me."

I hope that my son and other people's sons and daughters will find that to change human behavior, 100% of the results come from following Jesus' words on the most important commandment. "The greatest of the commandments is to love (You) with all (our) hearts and (our) neighbor as much as (we) love (ourselves)."

Whether the Pareto Principle is of your construction or not, wouldn't you be delighted if we lived our lives in a way that altered it just a bit?

Dear God: Were there hedges around the Garden of Eden?

When most people I know were still under age and had to listen to their parents, their parents at one time or the other told them, "If Jimmy jumped off a cliff, would you do it?" Of course, my parents and others' parents were referring to one of the worst statements a child can make when accused of a misdeed. "But, Jimmy lit the first match (threw dirt clods on the roof, tried to hit a baseball over the neighbor's house, etc.)."

At a football game last night, I witnessed a spectacle I wish I hadn't. I watched several thousand students at the University of Georgia, my *alma mater*, Jimmy apparently leading them, rush the field of play before the game was over. They later tore down both goalposts in celebration of victory. Only you know what these bright young minds were thinking. I can't imagine any of them were thinking at all.

The mob mentality that sparked this classless act came from elsewhere. It has become fashionable in college football this year to rush the field and tear down the goalposts after a big victory. In this case, the victory came against a team that had beaten my *alma mater* in ten straight games. Now, Georgia had beaten many teams over those years, but not this one.

These leaders of tomorrow took their cue from some other schools that play in the Southeastern Conference. One school's fans tore down the goalposts twice, once after winning its first game in twenty-two tries and the next week after winning its first conference game over the same span of time. Another school's fans tore down the goalposts as a way to vent their frustrations from watching their proud program stumble over the past few years and then win back some respect with a victory against a highly regarded opponent. A third school had a big win and followed suit.

I didn't understand it. As a student, I don't think I'd have understood. Tearing down goalposts in these instances was an admission of past failure. It was as if the students, and whoever else participated, wanted to say to the world, "Yep, we've been losers." What they should have added was, "And now we don't know how to act like winners."

I know there's much to be said in these cases about how dignity and respect don't seem to matter much in modern society. In another time, rushing the field against warnings not to do so and then tearing down the goalposts, would have been labeled disorderly conduct and destruction of public property. Some people don't respect tradition or institutions or the need to act with restraint anymore, and, when there's a few thousand of them versus a few hundred security personnel, the odds are in their favor, and they know it.

Maybe all of this was just an amusing sidebar to you. You see all sorts of behavior every day that's worse than what transpired. Maybe I was the one offended for little reason. I noticed in the stands around me that almost everyone else was also deeply offended by the lack of class this mob showed. Did the rest of the crowd sense that this act went beyond youthful fun?

To make things worse, my child saw my reaction to these invaders. I wish he hadn't. Maybe I suffered a reverse reaction to the same stimulus with results that weren't any better in his eyes.

I wanted to talk to you about what made Jimmy run onto the

field because his actions explain much about some of the fields I've run on in my lifetime without considering what I was doing, or perhaps thinking based on some criteria that wasn't valid. It wasn't the fact that Jimmy's friends were going to run onto the field and act like total animals. It was timing. Jimmy ran onto the field because all the circumstances around him led him to a decision he wouldn't have made at another point in time.

He spent all week listening to the buildup of the game through the media. All the talk at school that week was about the game. He called home during the week, and his dad wanted to talk about the game. School had been on for a few weeks, and the early thrill of seeing friends and starting back to the routine of classes was wearing off. Studying had become part of the routine again.

The game offered an escape.

Because three other schools in the Southeastern Conference had torn down goalposts in celebration of exceptional victories, someone floated the idea that Georgia's turn was coming up. The first win after ten losses in a row to the opponent was easily as good a reason as any of the other schools had for ripping down their respective goalposts.

ESPN was covering the game, and part of their coverage includes getting students out early to the stands. The excitement grew, and the talk about tearing down the goalposts grew with it.

But Jimmy, and the rest of the goalpost rushers, had a problem. They weren't wanted on the field.

Actually, they had a bigger problem. Between the stands and the playing surface were hedges that many considered a sacred part of the stadium, a symbol of its uniqueness dating back many decades. To reach the field, the hedges had to be scaled.

And scaled they were. At that point in time, any shots of courage Jimmy may or may not have taken were replaced by the adrenaline rush of being part of the mob. So the hedges were scaled even before the game ended. The goalposts hung on for life until the end of the game, and then Jimmy and his buddies because they hadn't expended whatever demon possessed them, turned on the hedges themselves, taking souvenirs of this sacred part of the stadium as trophies of their act.

You've seen many "hedges" torn up. I now know how you feel, or maybe I do. I was angered and sickened that something that was sacred in my football world could be torn apart by the very people who should have held those neatly trimmed rows as beyond their touch.

I think you would agree the earliest story of torn hedges occurred in the first book of the Bible. Adam and Eve had the run of their own beautiful stadium, except their piece of turf had more animals than just Bulldogs. You put something akin to hedges off limits, which in a moment of bad timing, they couldn't resist taking.

That must have put a kink in your plans for creation. You gave your very best, yet it wasn't enough. A victory over Tennessee wasn't enough for Jimmy and his friends either apparently. They had to demonstrate their temporary, but terrible power, to do something outside the lines.

Did Adam and Eve suffer from a decision made on its timing? The story of Adam and Eve doesn't deal with all of the particulars leading up to the decision for which all of us have been paying since. If the sin was in crossing the hedges, didn't the series of events that led up to that moment have an element of sin in it as well? I don't know many people who have done anything terribly wrong without something of ill, but less significant, consequence coming before it.

That's where timing comes in. I think some things happened along the way to move Adam and Eve toward their fateful decision. Maybe one or the other had a bad day. Perhaps boredom set in. Eve might have been thinking about how non-communicative Adam was, and Adam might have been thinking about what a whiner Eve turned out to be. In their mutual frustration, they bit, no pun intended, at something that appeared to offer a mild statement of rebellion against each other. And, of course, when we sin against each other, we've sinned against you as well.

It's in the major and inconsequential occurrences of each day that we are shaped toward making decisions. I think this is where you come into play. If you could help us stop to consider why we're about to do something against a broader picture of right and wrong for us and our neighbor, it might be we would make fewer poor decisions.

I might not have lost my temper in front of my son, which will be a bigger deal in his life long-term than anything those bozos did on the field, whether he consciously remembers or not. People might not shoot each other without thinking. Marriages might not be started or ended, resignations might not be tendered or jobs accepted without significant forethought. We might make all sorts of good decisions.

All of these good things we might do depend on waiting on you to show us the right thing for each of us. All of us today share something with Adam and Eve. When something we want is within our reach, we want to reach for it, whether we have to cross hedges we shouldn't cross or not.

I like the sanctity of those hedges as a shrine to football. I hope you'll help me see the sanctity that exists inside your purpose.

Dear God:
Do you like work?

If you do, is a favorable disposition toward this activity something you grant to a select few? Are certain people given a gene that drives them to succeed in their chosen profession?

Or, are the rest of us burn-outs?

I've decided I don't much like work. I used to like it a lot. Work gave me a sense of fulfillment. There were clear outcomes that I could look back on and recognize that, somewhere in the process, I made a difference.

Something happened along the way. I don't get it any more.

I was sitting in a meeting today. The meeting was one of these quarterly reporting and strategy type gatherings that most companies hold. The meeting brought in people from all over the company to talk about where we had been and where we were going.

I used to get excited about these gatherings. Knowing that I'd have some insightful thought that would make everyone pause for a second and think, "Hey, he's right," I always looked forward to these quarterly events. As I sat through parts of this one today, I realized the flame didn't burn as brightly anymore for me. I realized that the issues were the same issues that surfaced at other companies in other times, but rarely changed, no matter the fervor of the discussion.

Fortunately, for the sake of this event, other people are ready to take my place in the discussion—people convinced of the rightness of their convictions, ready to go to the wall to prove their point. I realized that I've become one of the guys who used to sit quietly for the most part, recognizing they'd heard the same discussions ten or twenty years before. Looking back, they knew the answers to the questions I fought so hard to answer. They, also, realized the odds of change occurring weren't good.

I retreated to my office as much as possible, much easier to do when you don't have much to offer in the course of the discussion. I managed to miss close to half of the afternoon session. The problem, if it is a problem, is that I went back to my office and didn't exactly change the bottom line there either.

Tomorrow brings the next half day of the meeting, and I'm wondering if there's much point. As a matter of fact, I have the first forty-five minutes in the morning to say whatever it is I want to say and I ought to be well-prepared to promote and defend my part of the plan, but I don't think it's worth it. Had I thought so earlier today, I would have spent the time away from the meeting putting together some nice graphics, developing a strategy to win over the doubters, and, in general, trying to leave people with the impression that I had my act together.

While it's not an act in literal terms, what I do everyday is an act in the sense of what it actually accomplishes. I'm afraid I've been around long enough now to realize that I can make a difference, but it's a diluted difference, rarely representative of the time and effort invested to make that difference.

I've reached the conclusion that you must infect some people with a work gene; people determined that they are going to make a difference if it kills them. I'm sure there's some basic psychology in all of this, some need to prove their smarts, power, resourcefulness, and cunning.

If I ever had the work gene, I think I've lost it to the point that I need to throw myself on your mercy and hang it up. As you know, I've already asked my wife if I could quit, and she, in a moment she's likely to regret, said, "If that's what you think you need to do." I call that blanket permission. I don't know what you call it.

Should I? Would it get me off dead center to have 'the talk' in the morning? Might I get a little more enthusiastic about life if I knew that I was living on the edge? Would you provide for me, given what you know about my frustrations?

I don't know the answer. I wish you'd tell me.

Maybe you already have.

Let's go back to the original question. Do you like work? I recognize you did the ultimate work of all time, literally, in the process of creation. I've worked in the engineering and construction business for fifteen years, and I've never heard anyone claim to have designed and constructed the universe though I've known quite a few who acted as if they did.

The Bible states you rested on the seventh day. You were finished with your work. I'm not finished, but I'm tired. I'm not physically tired. I'm just tired of it. Mentally tired. Emotionally drained. I have a decade and seven years until I can start drawing from my IRA.

The Bible further states that we were your final act of creation. People. Did bringing us into being make you stop for a day to ponder what might come of this particular part of your work? Or, was your rest simply stopping to enjoy the magnificence of the view? There's something about stopping at the end of the day to admire something good your work has accomplished.

But what happens when you can't seem to find any joy in the fruits of your labor? What happens when it all seems so purposeless, but it has to be purposeful if anything of consequence is to be gained from it? You don't have the need for a paycheck.

You're sort of like "old money" types that work because they want to, not because they need to.

What I'd really like to get and what many other people would like to get out of work is the feeling that we matter. We don't mind the money either. But after a point the money isn't of great consequence because we'll spend it all anyway. What we have left is work.

How does work feel for you today? You've gotten creation behind you, but now you have the responsibility for six billion lives, which is 5,999,999,998 more than you had on the day before you took that first break. There has to be some effort required with that much responsibility.

Let's stop and think about it for a minute. You created nature, and there's a natural order to it so that things run pretty much on their own. But there's little order in the way people live unless it's ordered chaos of some sort. You must be busier now than you were before. Don't you get tired of the same old problems resurfacing constantly?

If you don't get tired of it, you must feel some sense of purpose. Is that correct? You still find a reason every day to put out your best effort.

How do people like me who just can't find a good reason, other than putting food on the table and a roof over our heads, keep on keeping on?

One thing of which I'm becoming more certain is you've just about talked me out of hanging it up in the morning, but then you've known me a while. Please note, however, that I don't want to keep going through this endless cycle of discouragement. It's the same things I heard ten years ago. I don't think the answers are going to change.

Is there something you want to change about me?

Dear God:
Have you rained down
any toads lately?

You remember the TV series *WKRP*? I've seen reruns lately. There's a character on one of the episodes called Reverend "Little Ed" Pembrooke. Reverend Little Ed, in addition to being a former wrestler, was vaguely familiar with the plagues described in Exodus and offered to "rain down toads" on the station if his show was pulled for using his rented airtime to sell such items as "The Dead Sea Scrolls Steak Knives" or the "Sermon on the Mount Shower Curtain."

Station management was more afraid of Little Ed and his physical largesse than the threat of toads, but it made me think about plagues and threats of plagues in our world today. If you were going to really sock it to us, would you actually use toads?

Little Ed wasn't exactly accurate with his threat. The Bible records that you caused the toads to come up out of the Nile, much easier to envision than toads being rained down from above. In either case, I'm not sure toads are a modern solution. Because we retreat to the safety of office buildings, plants, and completely conditioned houses and go from one place to another in cars, toads wouldn't be near the nuisance they were to the people of Egypt though I imagine the mess on the Interstate wouldn't be pretty.

You might also consider that there are animal rights groups today who would be more aghast over the unauthorized use of toads outside their natural habitat than the significance of your sending them in such a spectacular fashion. You'd be in court before you knew it. Everyone would have to step around the toads to get there, of course, but such flippant use of animals wouldn't be tolerated. The old-fashioned stuff isn't the way to go in sending plagues in our direction.

So don't send any toads, locusts, or gnats. I'm just suggesting that times have changed and that to attract real attention will take a different approach than pesky members of the animal kingdom.

Since Little Ed brought it up, I thought it might be worth a visit to Exodus to gain some perspective on the plagues used to free the people of Israel from Egypt. I noticed that you brought some pretty nasty stuff the way of the Egyptians.

The Bible appears to be unequivocal about Pharaoh's willingness to give up after you laid it to him a few times. The Bible says that you changed Pharaoh's mind, "hardened his heart," because you weren't yet ready to have this display of your power end. You didn't want the people of Egypt, or perhaps, more importantly, the people of Israel to forget.

I have to be up-front with you since you already know I'm thinking it; reading that you manipulated the situation didn't give me the most comforting feeling. I just don't think of you as being, well, devious. Then again, you were dealing with someone who thought he was you so it was a fair contest I suppose.

If you do need to attract our attention as much as you needed to get Pharaoh's, I have a few suggestions that aren't Biblical but would sure hit home today. Be warned. These particular plagues wouldn't take much effort on your part. I wouldn't want your thinking I doubted your ability by suggesting such simple solutions. Our lives are so confused and so interconnected to so many things that it won't take much.

· Constantly interrupt Internet service. There are people who rarely leave their homes because the Internet allows them to stay inside. The toads aren't going to give them one bit of pause. Take away this window to the world, however, and you have serious emotional crises going on in many lives.

· Make all of the women in the next James Bond movie dirt ugly. Most men, including me, might begin to think that Bond's lifestyle isn't that glamorous after all.

· Have all day traders only trade between three and four in the morning. All of us might learn to see that short-term gains aren't the goal in life.

· Turn all of the fast-food emporiums into turnip greens and cornbread establishments. People true to you will immediately see the purity of this change and embrace it. Of course, most of the children in our nation will have to learn to eat better or starve.

· If you want to hit people where it really hurts, close down the Krispy Kremes and see what happens.

· If you want to hit me where it hurts, put all of college football on probation: no scholarships, no television, no bowl games. I might find more productive things to do with autumn Saturdays, but somehow I doubt it.

· Immediately silence the tongue of anyone who speaks the words *synergy*, *mandate*, *liberal*, *conservative*, *consensus*, *bipartisan*, *coalition*, or *litigate*. The rest of us might use the awesome silence to consider you and how you want your world to run.

You see, we don't respond the same way as the people of old. They were close to the land. We're close to the conveniences of life. We want quick results with no pain, no deep thought, no dedication to anything long-term.

I don't want you to send plagues. I really don't. But, I wouldn't mind if you got our attention in any of the ways I've suggested. It would change *my* life.

If you do decide to send a few surprises our way, please don't forget that most of us don't think we're Pharaoh. One or two plagues ought to be enough to loosen up our hard hearts.

Dear God:
Do you believe in miracles?

If the sun didn't come up tomorrow, would you consider it a great and terrible thing? I can tell you how we'd feel. We wouldn't think it was great. It would certainly be terrible—an act far beyond our control and well out of the normal course of life as we know it.

If the sun came up, but we learned that a great asteroid was bearing down on us with the power to put us into years of darkness and perhaps extinction, would the last minute diversion of that asteroid away from the earth be considered a cause for rejoicing?

Thus, a miracle is born.

You've heard the old expression, "Beauty is in the eye of the beholder." Well, so are miracles, at least to my thinking. For some extraordinary act to be called a miracle, someone must first believe that it was. And it must be good. Saving the earth from destruction is good, pretty close to unsurpassably good, but it's not the extraordinary thing we hope for daily. We hope instead that the bumps in our lives will be smoothed in some way.

Since you are generally the source credited for miracles, I think it's important to know if you believe that miracles happen. Hear me out, please. I don't mean to be disrespectful. It's just that it

217

seems as the Big Beholder, you might not have the same perception about acts most of us would call miraculous.

We like miracles.

We like using the word miracle to explain anything that defies ready explanation. Since you can explain anything, you might not see miracles the same way as people. Of course, as the generally acknowledged source of miracles, you know which were acts of intervention on your part and which were coincidence.

But, then, you might not believe in coincidence.

Here's the problem. We like miracles so much that it's hard to tell when a miracle starts and some highly unusual, but not impossible, act occurs.

One of the most famous utterances of the word miracle came in 1980 from a sportscaster named Al Michaels. Just using the word turned him from a fine, but relatively unknown sportscaster, into a national icon. He exclaimed, "Do you believe in miracles?" as the American Olympic hockey team knocked off the previously invincible Soviet team. The entire nation, even those of us who knew little about hockey, wanted to believe that good triumphs, that the underdog wins. We wanted to believe the Evil Empire could be slain. And it was.

Mr. Michaels coined the perfect phrase to help us believe. That hockey victory wasn't a miracle. It was as good as one. That victory had the same effect on American psyches as David's centering a sling-shot propelled pebble onto Goliath's forehead with the velocity and effect of a large-caliber rifle did for the army of Israel. Our side won.

We like miracles. They change our lives.

I don't know how you see this whole idea of your intervention. Is a miracle something you improvise, or is it part of the plan? If you can see out into the future and understand everything that's going to happen, is a miracle a miracle to you, or is it just part of moving toward the inevitable? If you're simply executing the plan you already have in place, I wouldn't think you'd consider any acts on your part as miracles.

If there's a cast-in-heavenly granite plan and we're just being moved around as part of it, we can't possibly know the plan though many have tried to predict on your behalf. Without knowledge of your intent, we see the daily grind as lacking specific examples of your presence and of your power.

Miracles are our reminder.

If there's no cast-in-place plan and deviations and exceptions are the rule, miracles *are* a big deal. Miracles are an answer to our plea, sometimes to pleas we never even made.

Remember: We like miracles.

If you dropped in on 100 church services today where the average member could say what's on their mind aloud during the course of the service, you'd hear about some miracles you performed. These miracles would range from a wayward dog that returned home after three days to the absence of cancer where there once was much.

Miracles encompass a broad range for us.

You directed the dog back home. You cleansed cancer from the body. The miracle is in the eye of the beholder, just as it is from your perspective. The difference? You know which one you made happen. We can only guess by degrees.

But, then, you might have made both happen.

According to the Bible, all "good and perfect" gifts come from you. Aside from being a bit redundant in phrasing, that verse says a great deal about what we should expect from you. What it says is that we should only expect the best.

That idea gets preached a great deal, so credit is being given to you. But those same people want miracles when they don't get the best. They want someone, that someone being you, to step in and intervene when the dog hasn't come back home and the cancer grows instead of disappearing. People want to trust you as long as the right answer comes their way.

When the right answer doesn't come, many decide to trust you even more, the most miraculous of miracles. Sometimes we find that not getting the answer we wanted raises an answer of a different kind.

That answer is you.

We'll keep looking for those answers from you. We'll look anywhere we can put our finger on one. In more than a few of our lives, you're one big tabloid newspaper. Instead of "Satan's Skeleton Found" featuring a picture of a human skull with cow horns stuck on each side, we want to hear, "Woman Hit In Head By Foul Ball Regains Sight."

I know you are attuned to present-day culture. You've noticed that we will go quite some distance to create an impression of supernatural intervention. Something sends the wind to rattle the cornstalks in a field on a calm day and follows with a quiet but distinct, "Build it, and they will come."

A movie takes one out of the park in our collective longing.

Of course, you weren't credited with that one; it's left to the viewer's imagination as to whom the speaker of those words might be, to whom the great hand that guided Kevin Costner's journey belonged. But that's the kind of thing we expect from you.

Miracles establish your credentials with us.

We've grown to understand from the pages of the Bible that you regularly performed miracles during biblical times. Jesus established his credentials by turning water into wine. He provided a few other great story lines along the way as well.

When Jesus left the earth, the early church became multiple hues of bilingual as part of its coming of age. The greatest writer of the early church came to you after being blinded as he walked down the road.

Were the people of that time just closer to the source? Only you know that answer.

I do know that not many years after those great acts occurred the church had to be reminded that faith is "the hope for things unseen." Those folks were looking for miracles, too.

Are miracles a thing of the past?

We still want to believe even when we don't, well, believe. Many of us are still looking for the answer even when the answer doesn't seem likely. Faith healers pack modern coliseums. A slap on the head, a gust of breath in the face are enough to cure, to heal—enough to heal someone who wants to believe.

That's what you're about, aren't you?

You want us to believe. And whether we're sophisticated or simple, believing in the particular way our individual spirits are capable of believing is the path toward the miracle of you.